I0391080

A Collection of Mandalas

A Color Therapy Coloring Book

BY

Kim Jordan Blair

I want to thank Kimberly Davidson for allowing me to use her colored version my Flower mandala on the cover.

I also want to thank Renee Kritzer for allowing me to use her colored version of my dragon eye mandala on the cover.

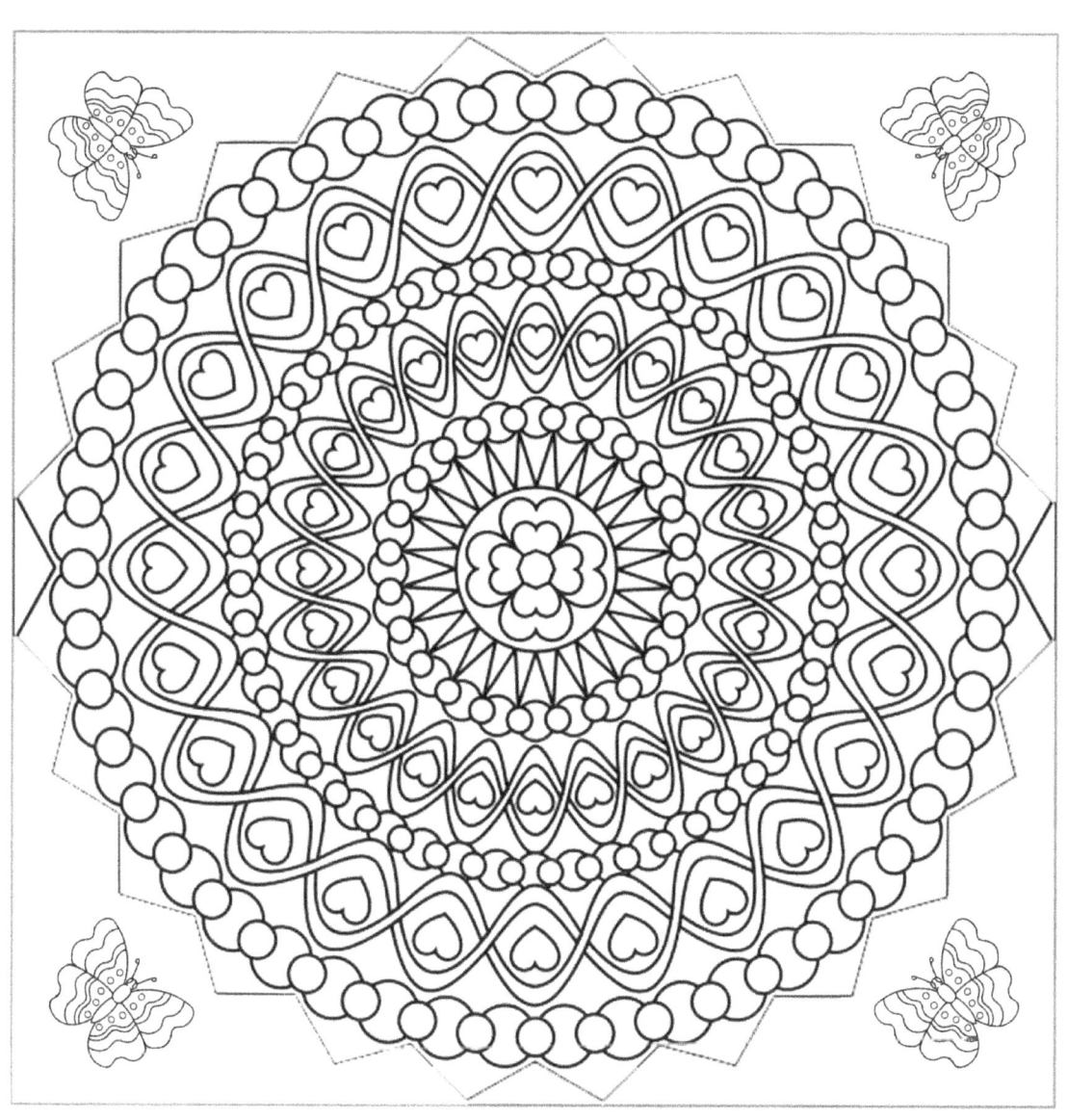

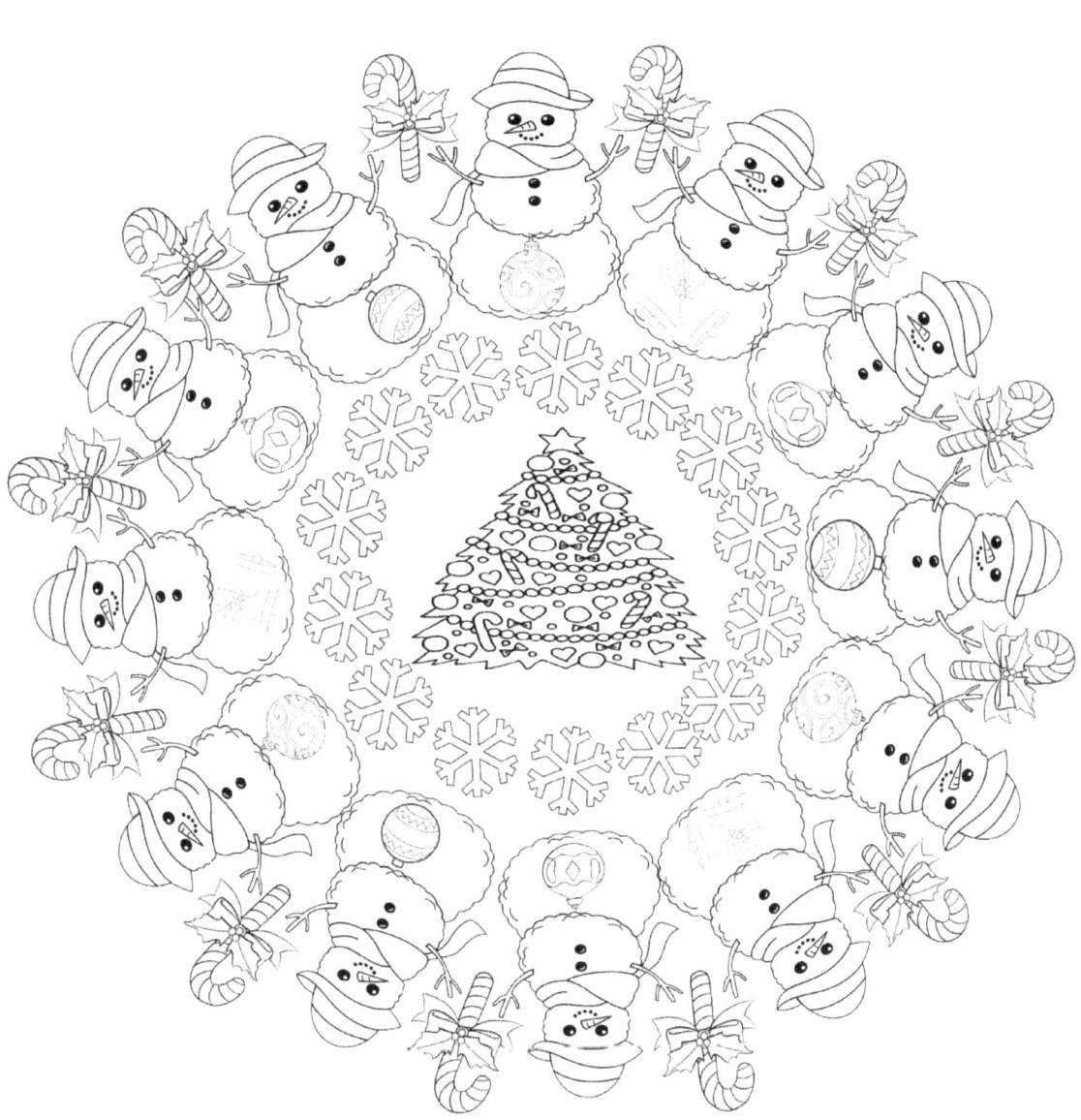

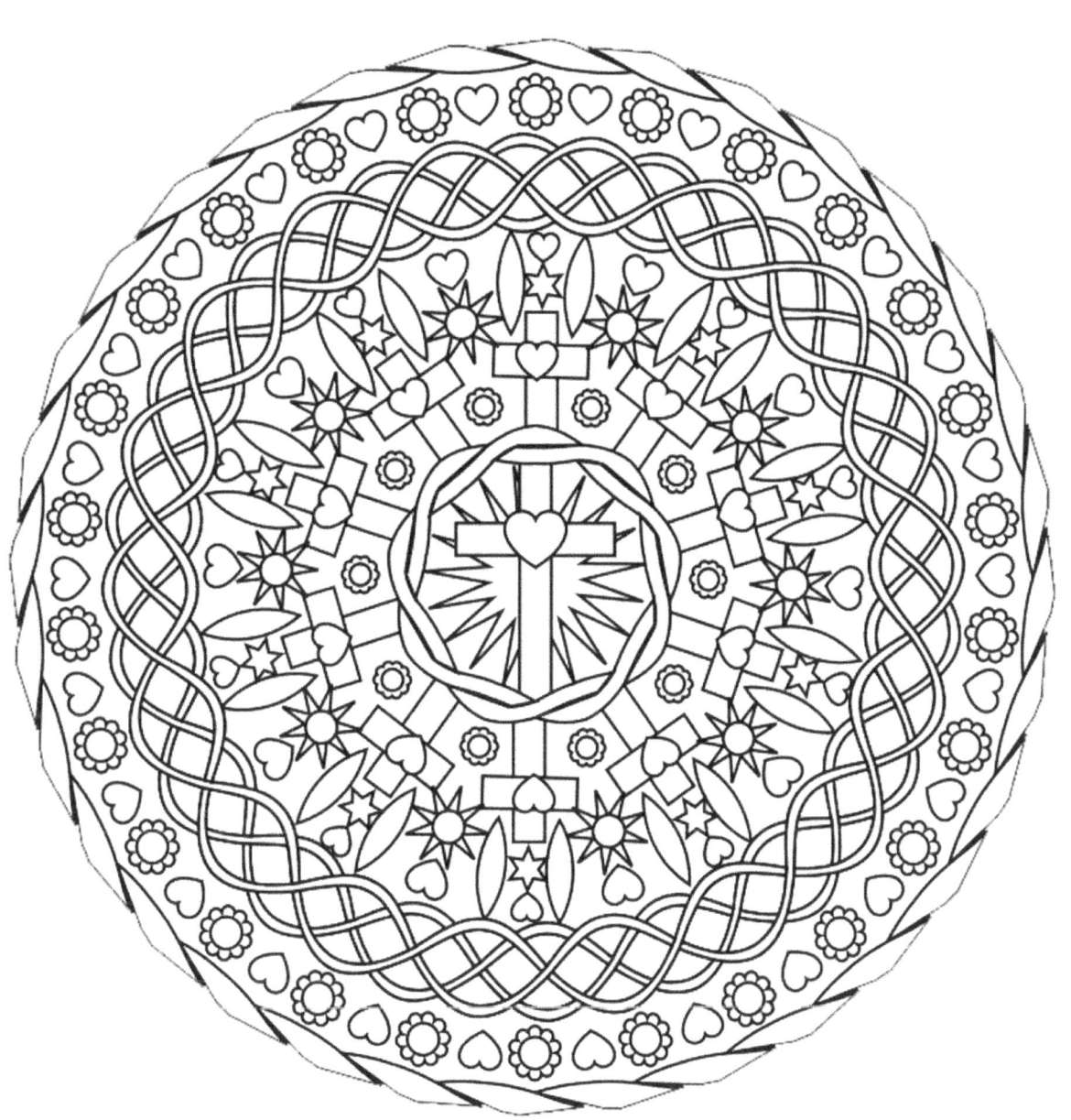

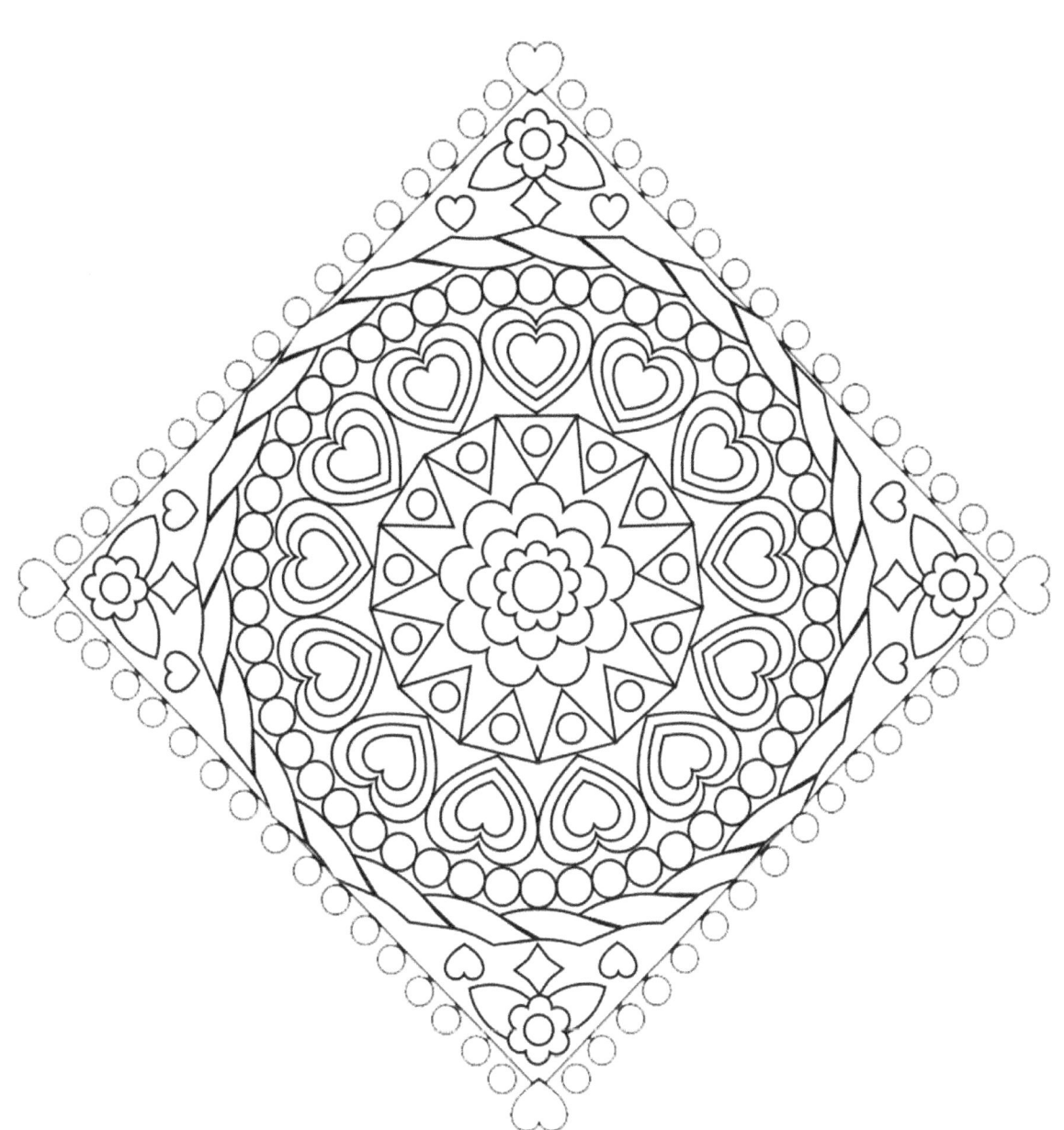

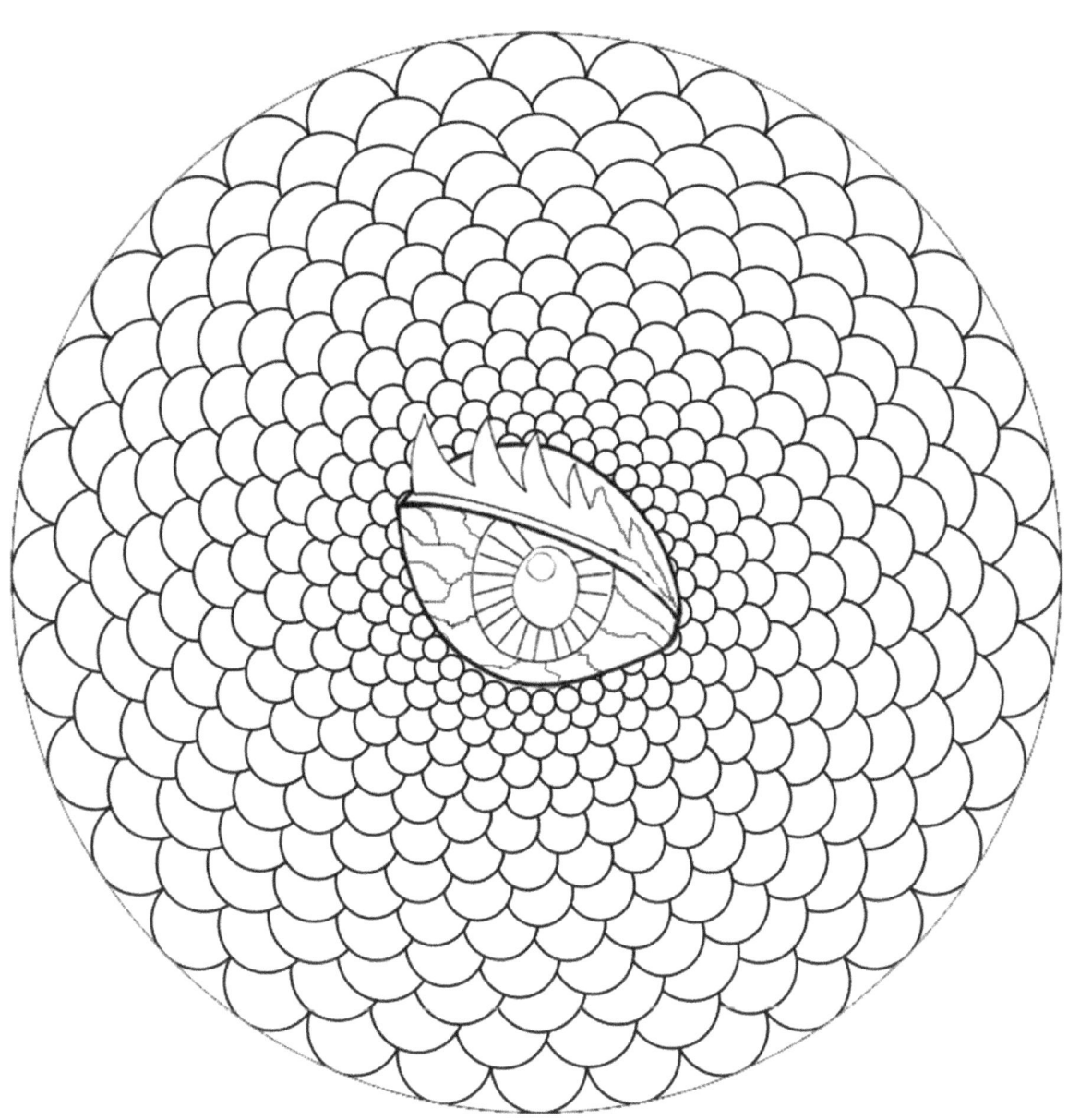

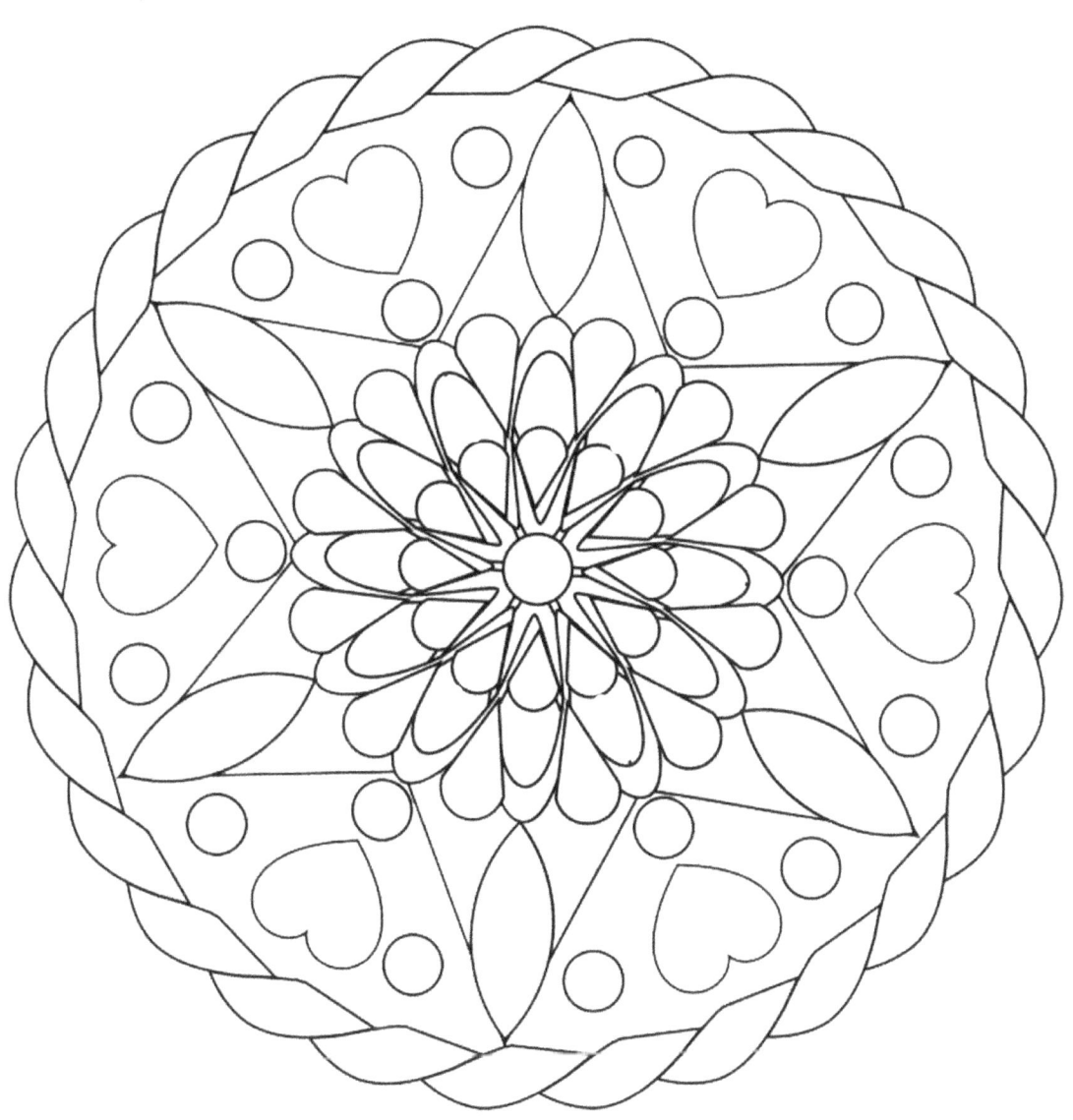

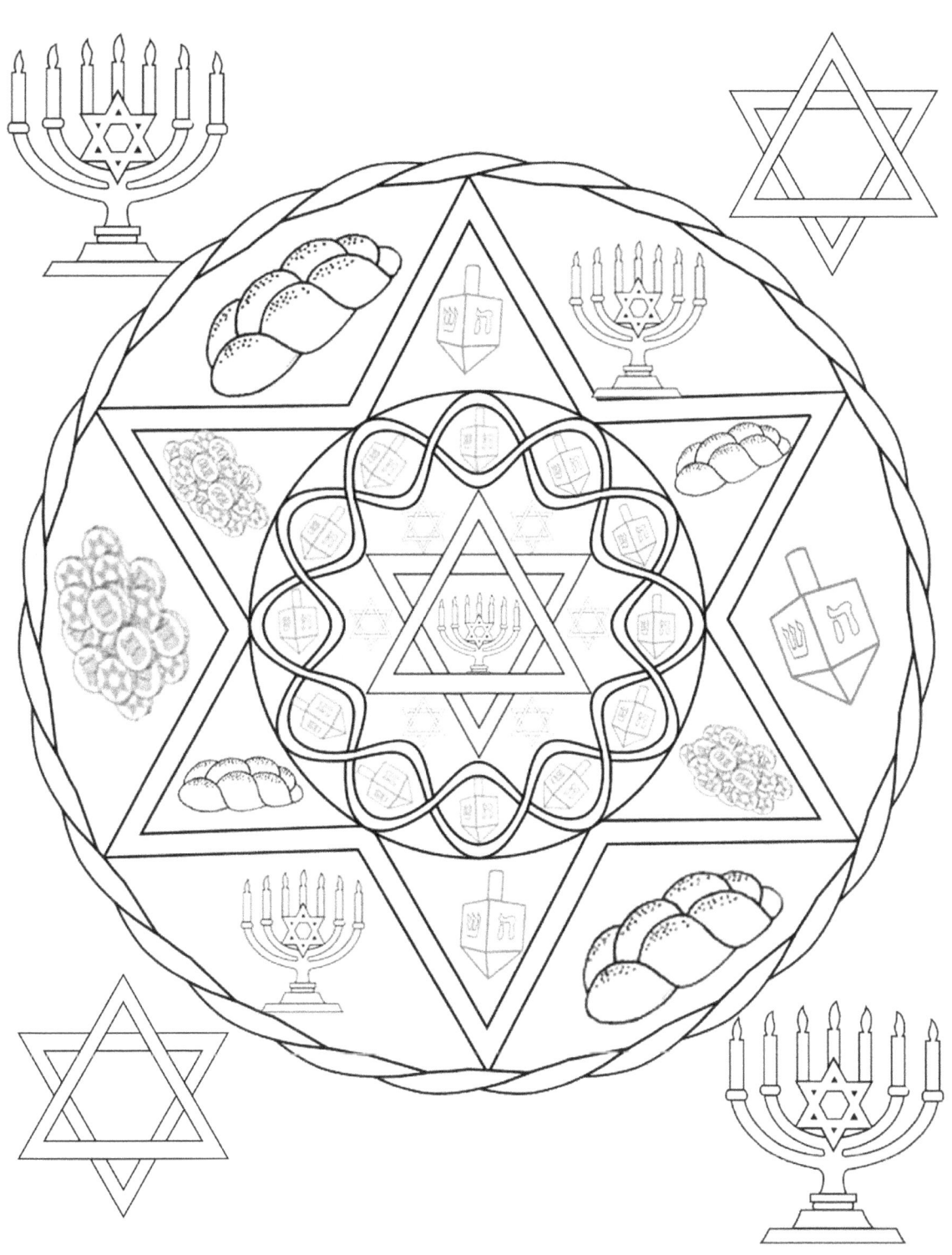

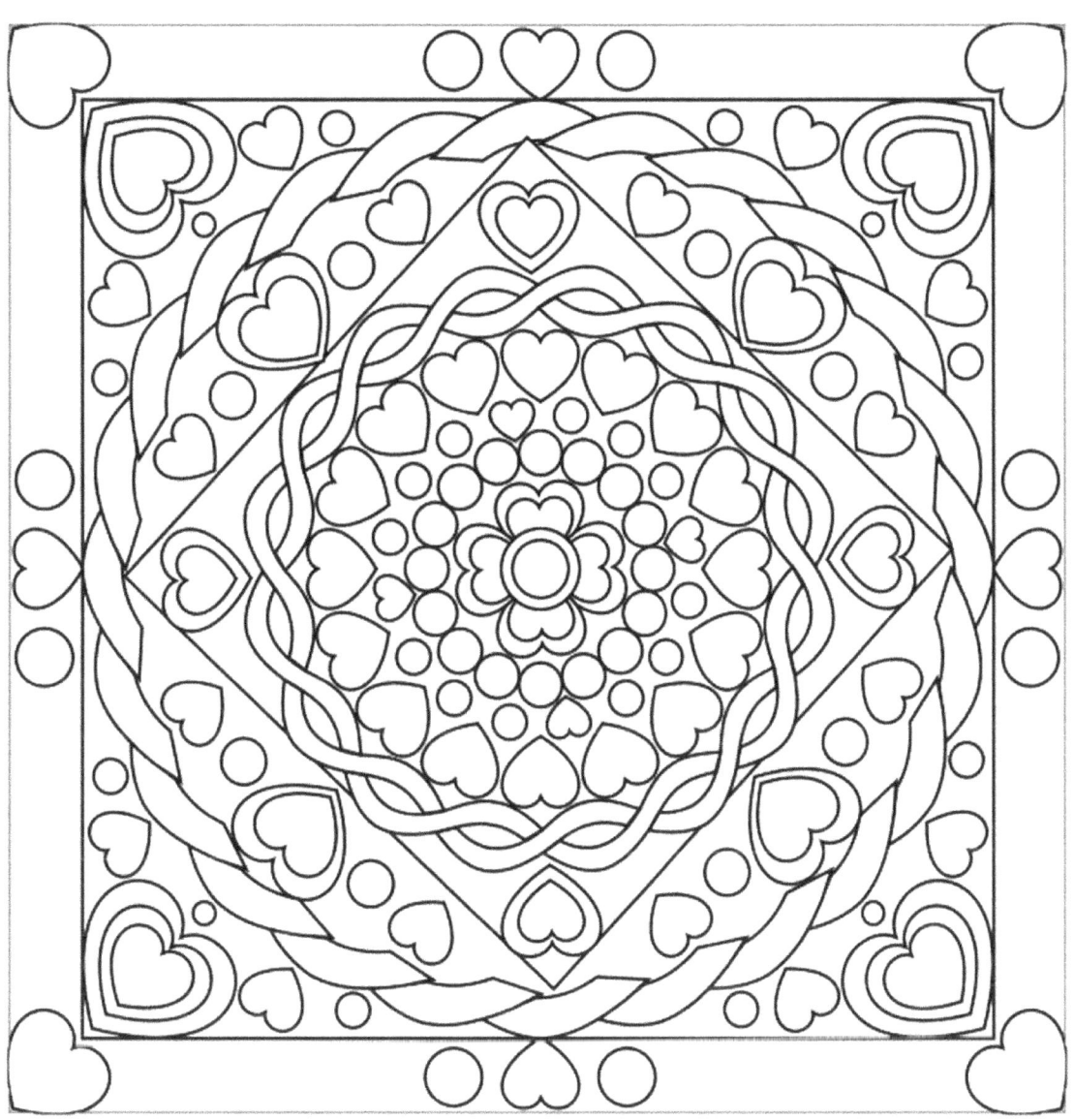

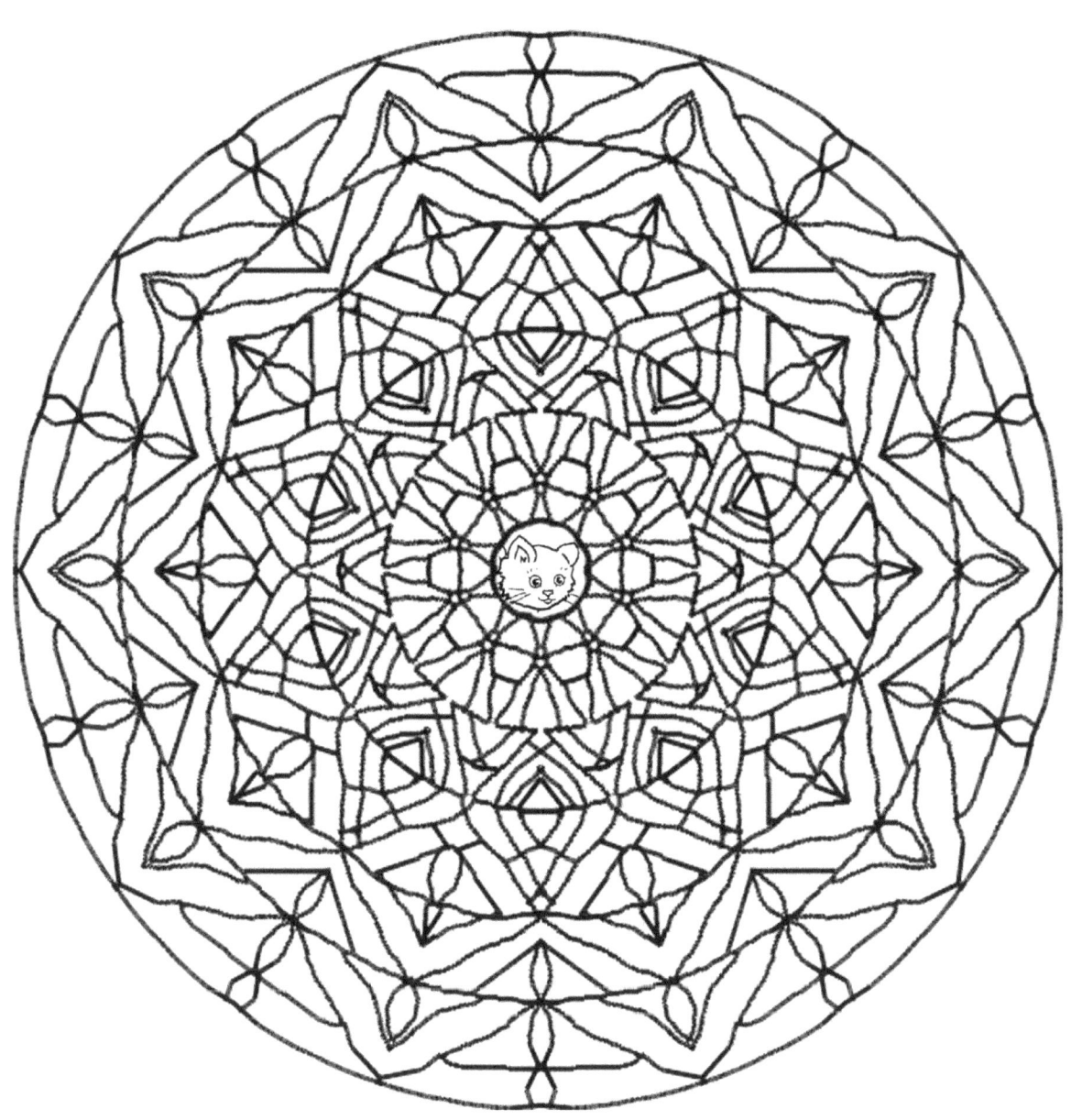

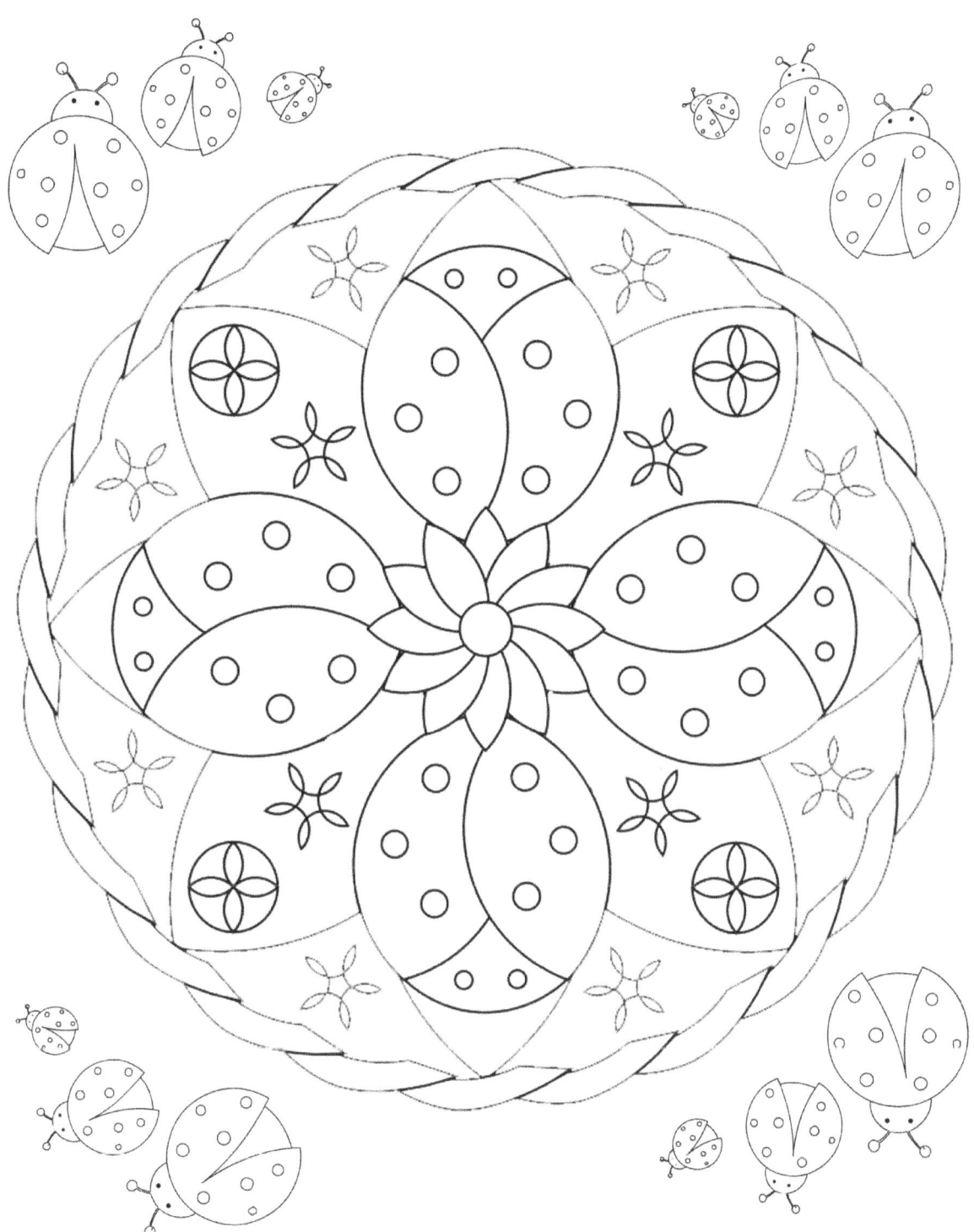

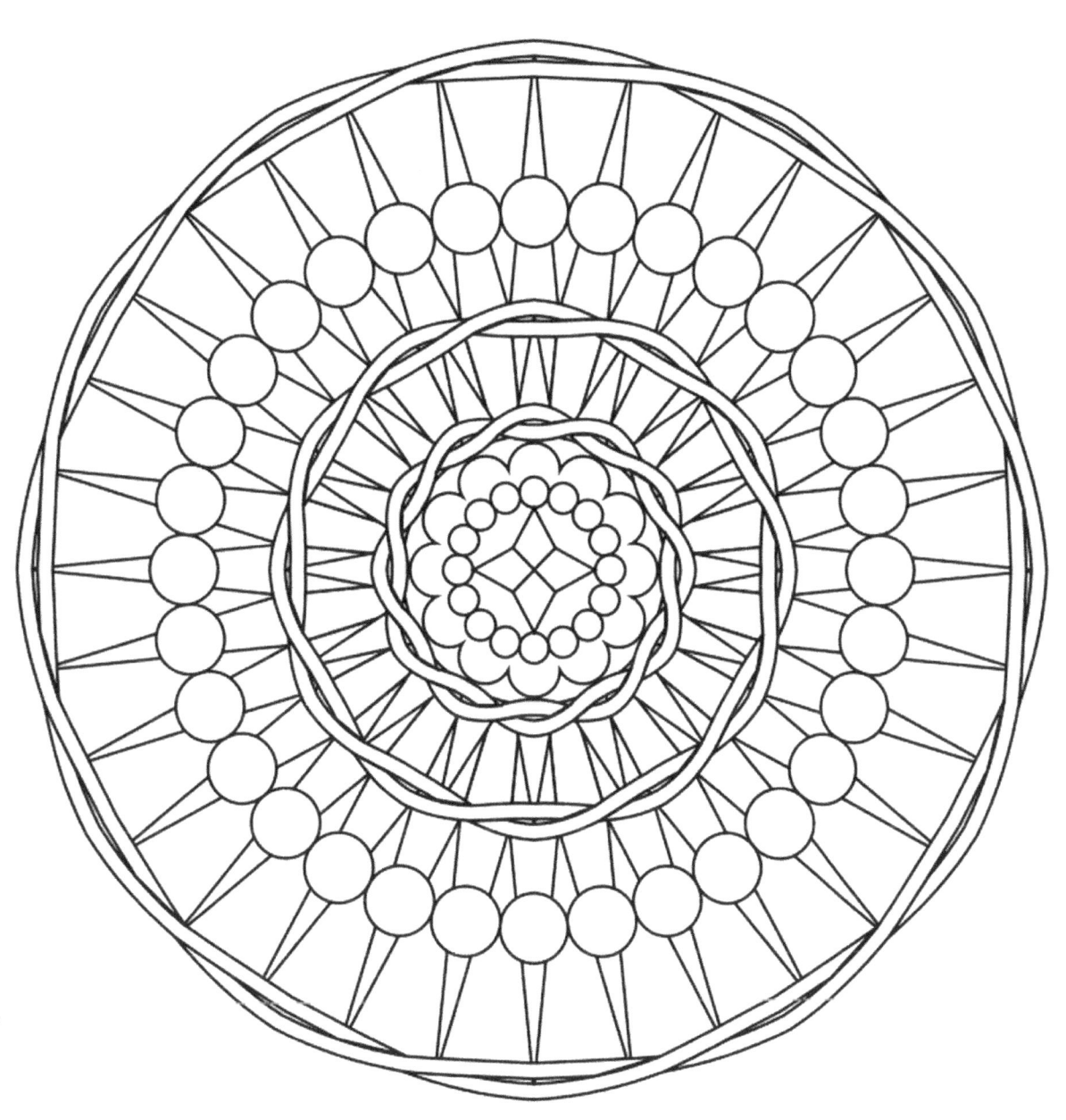

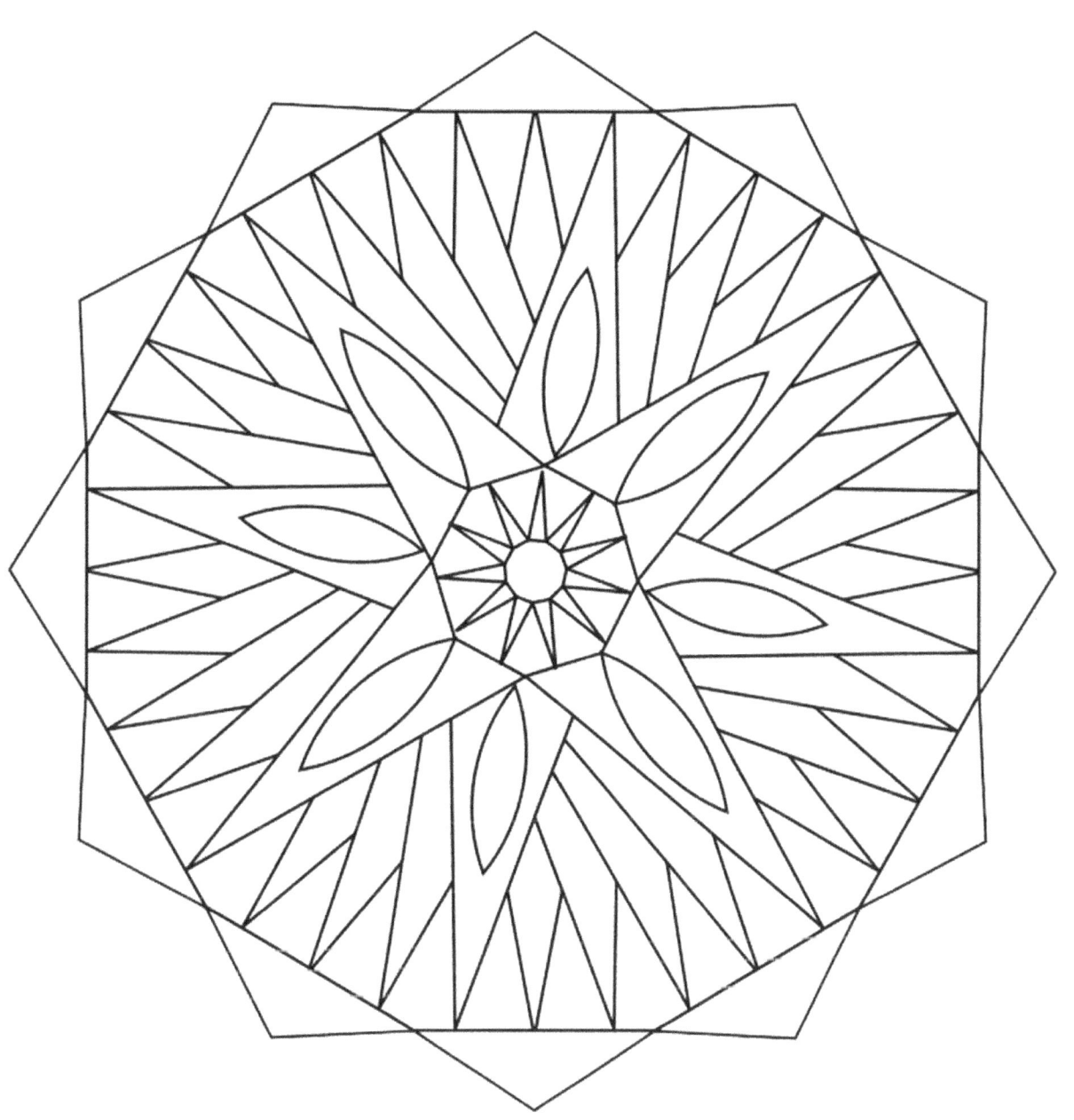

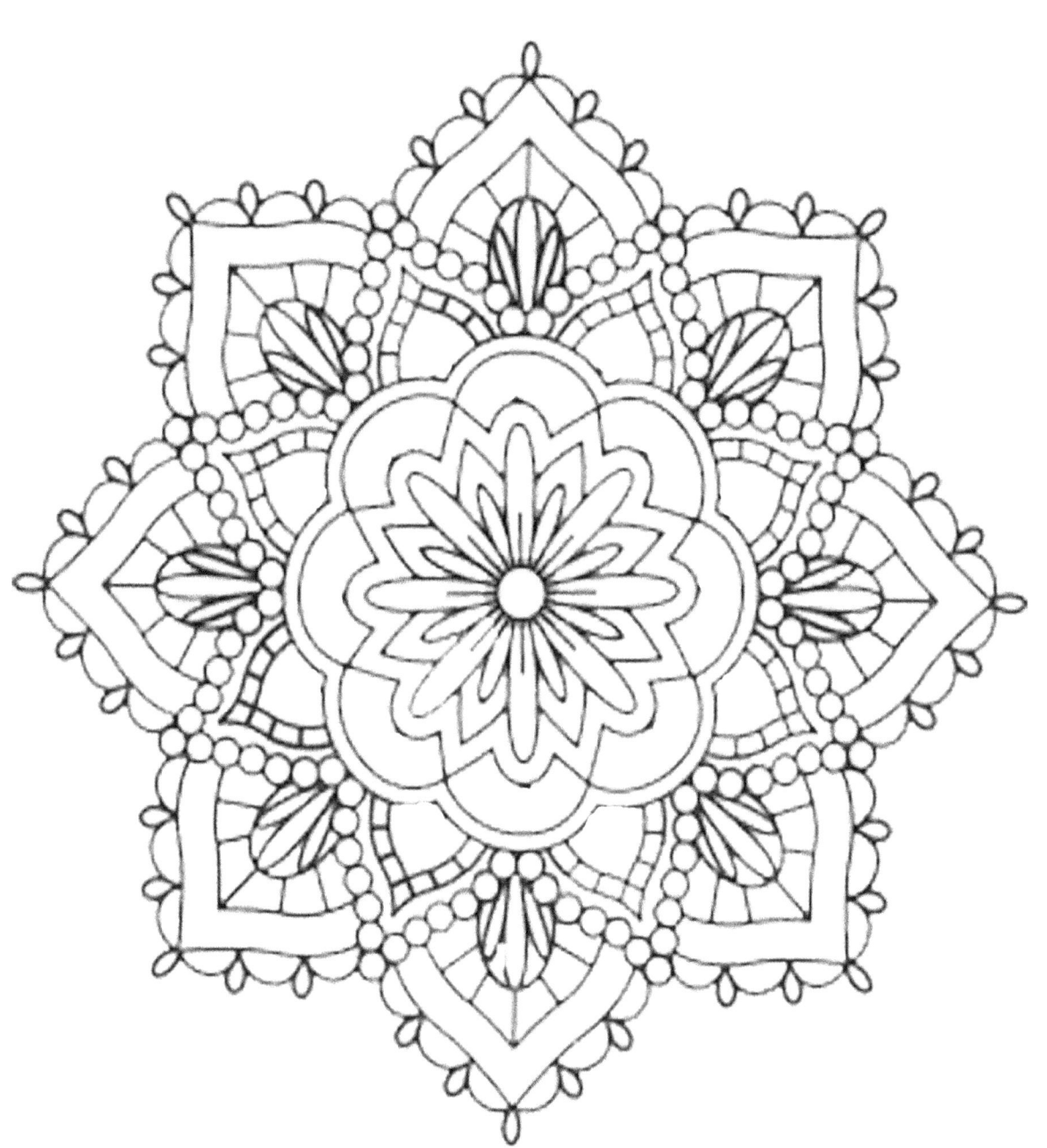

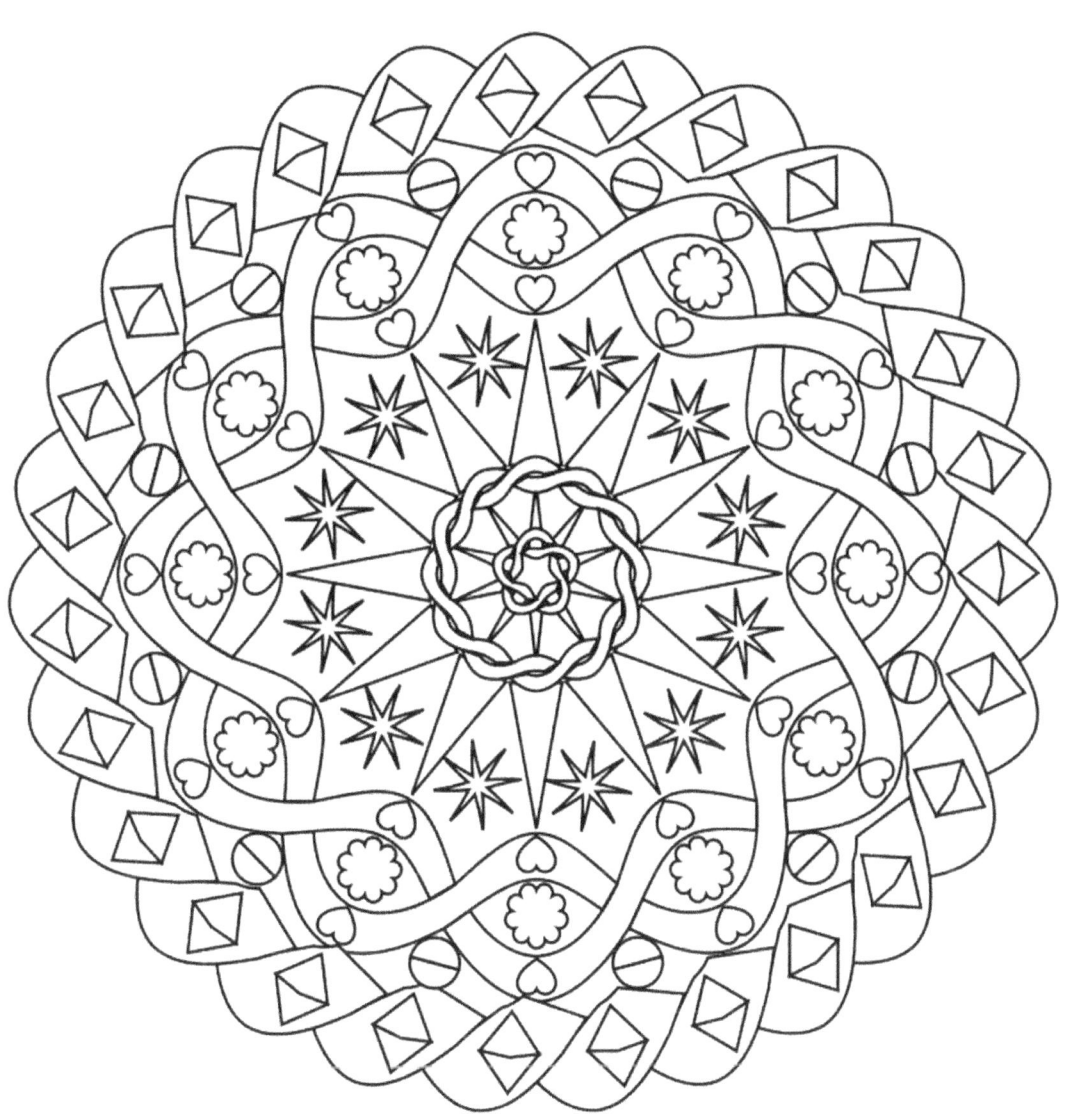

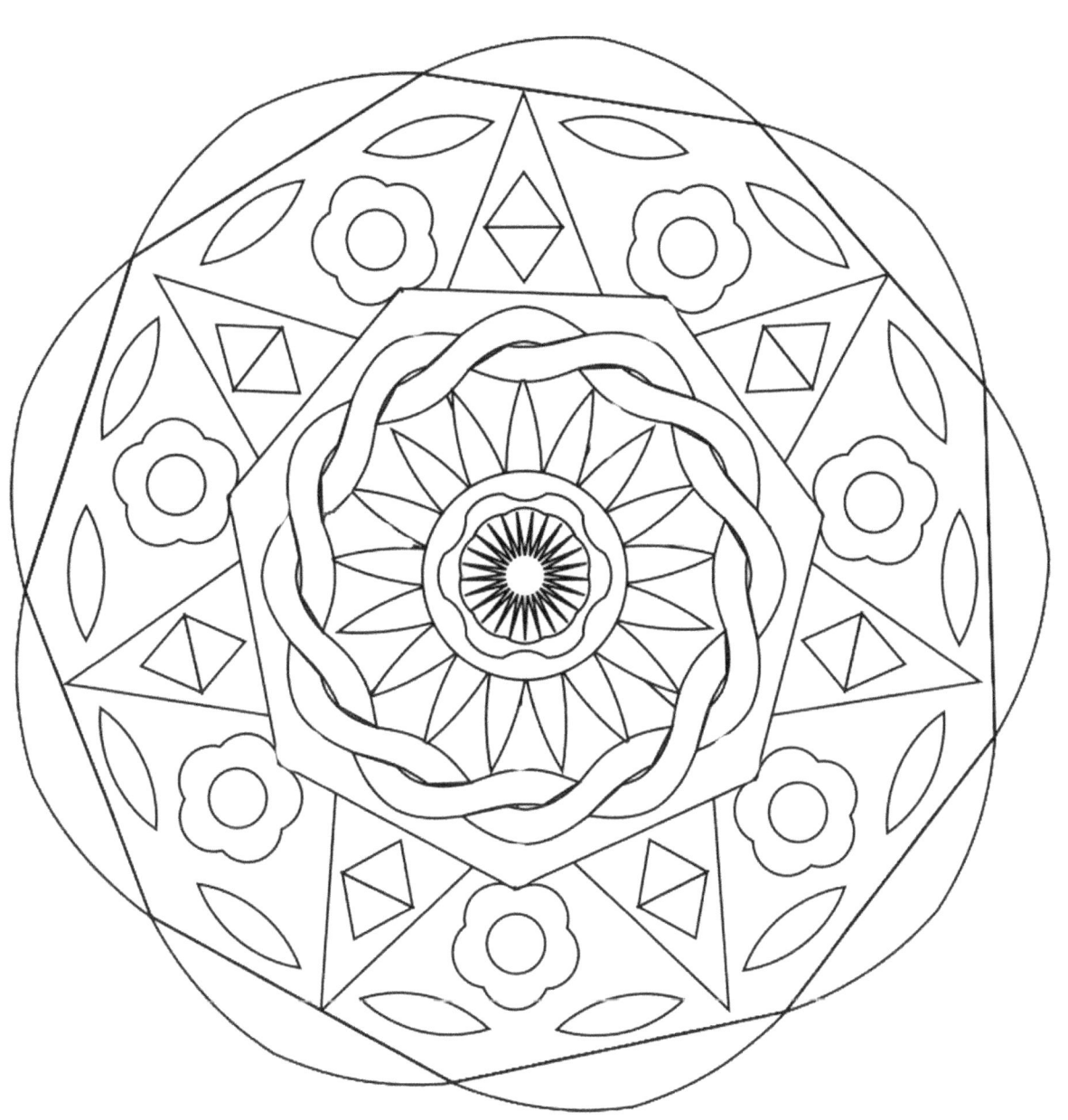

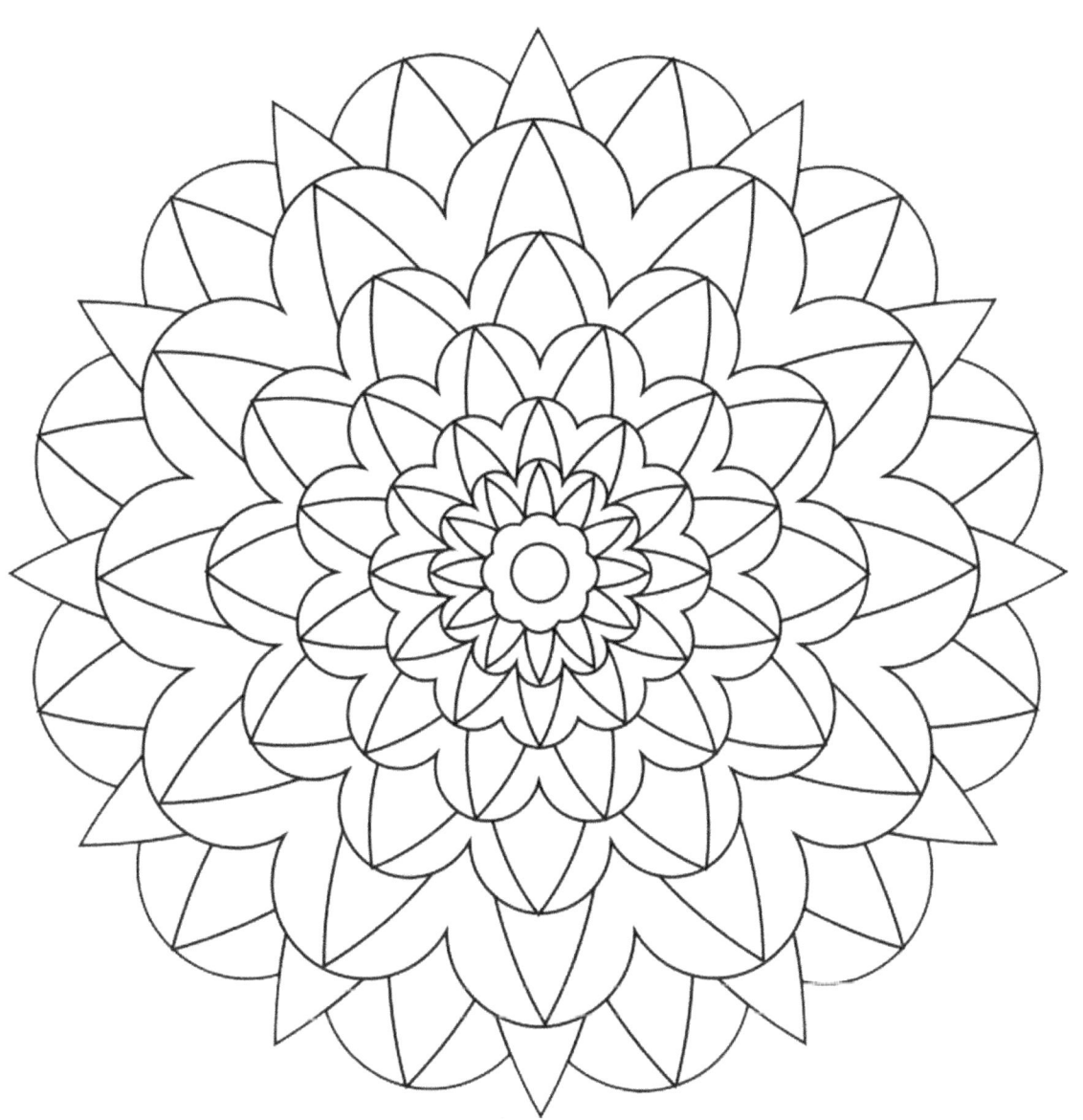

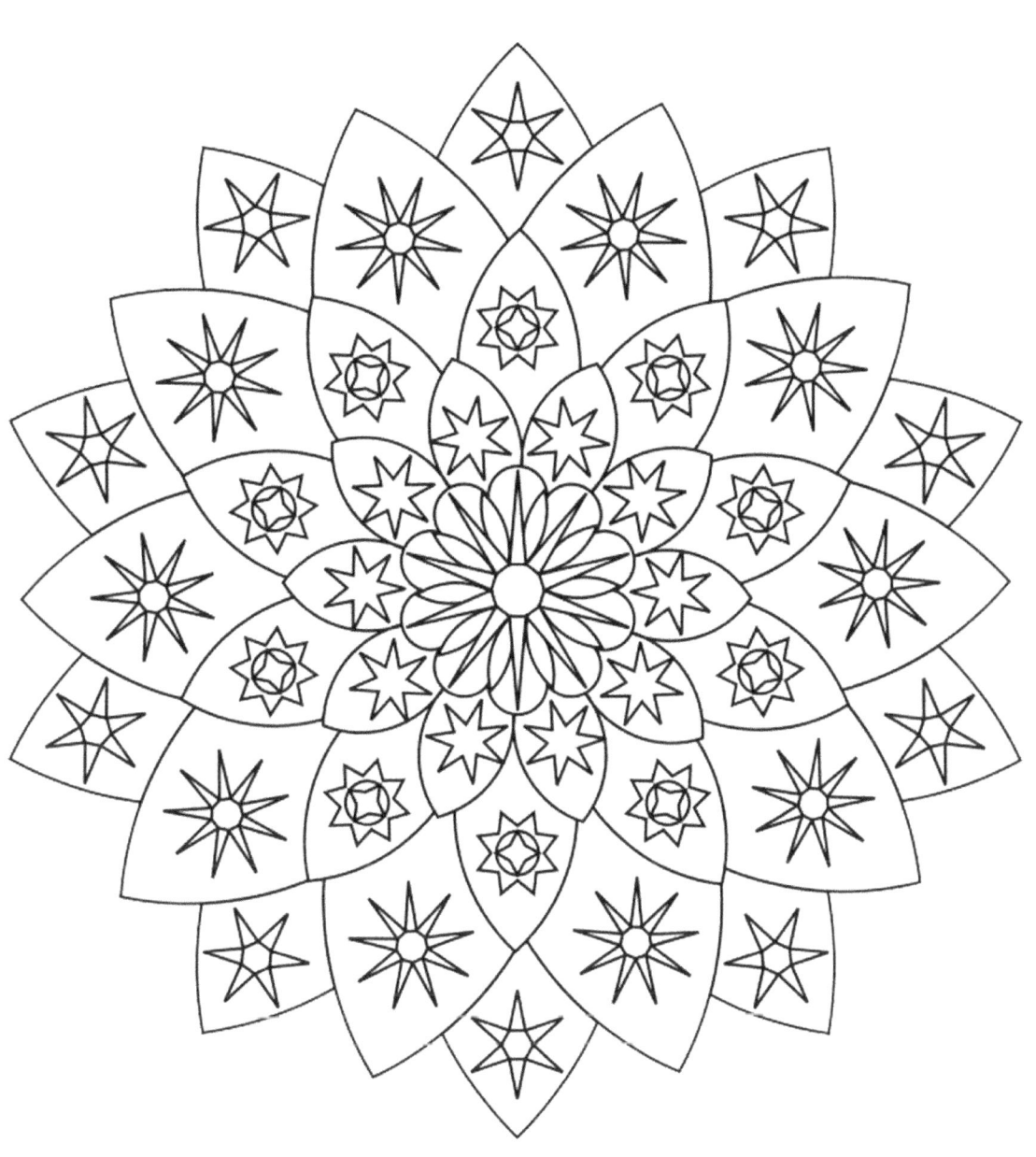

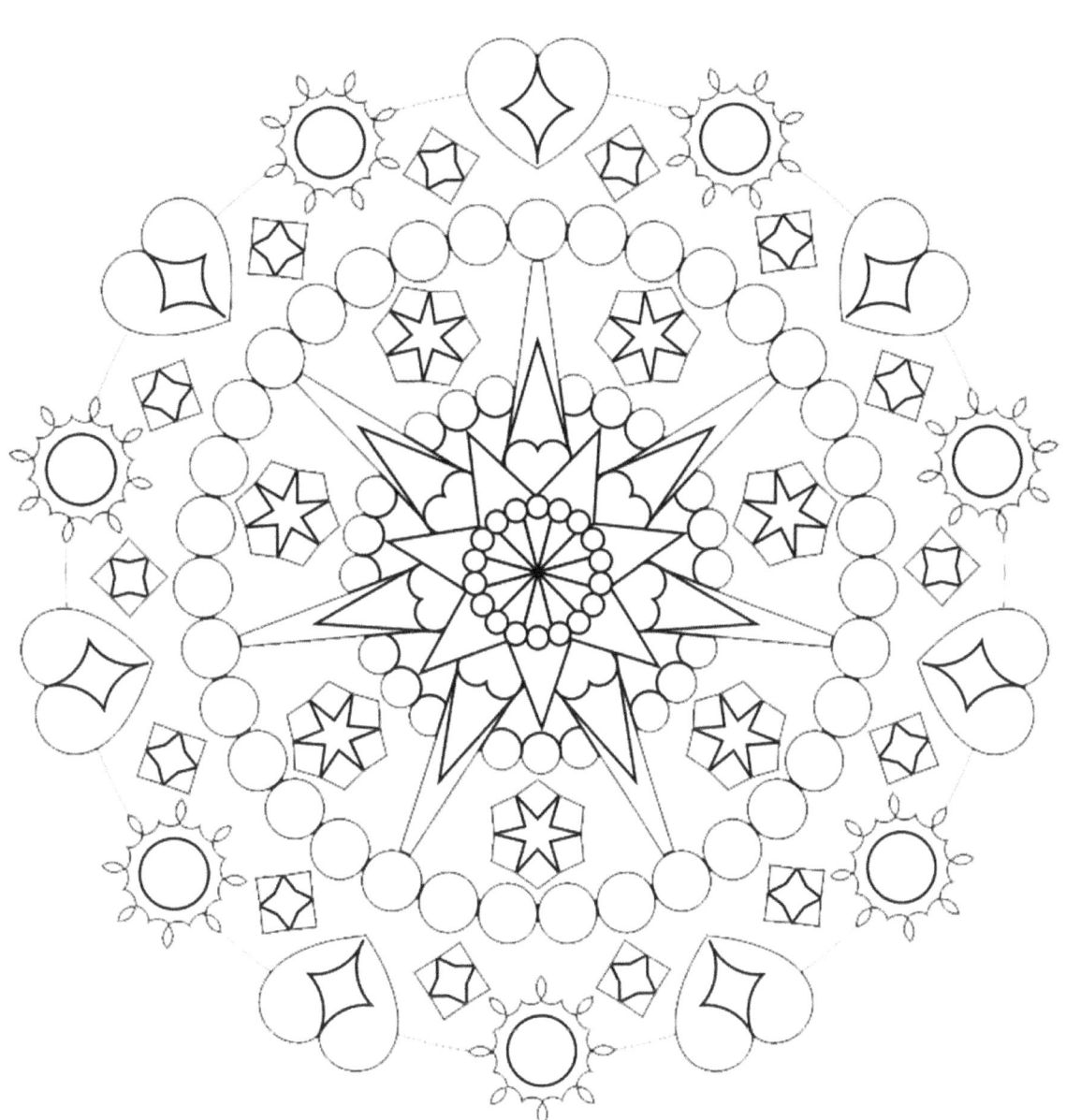

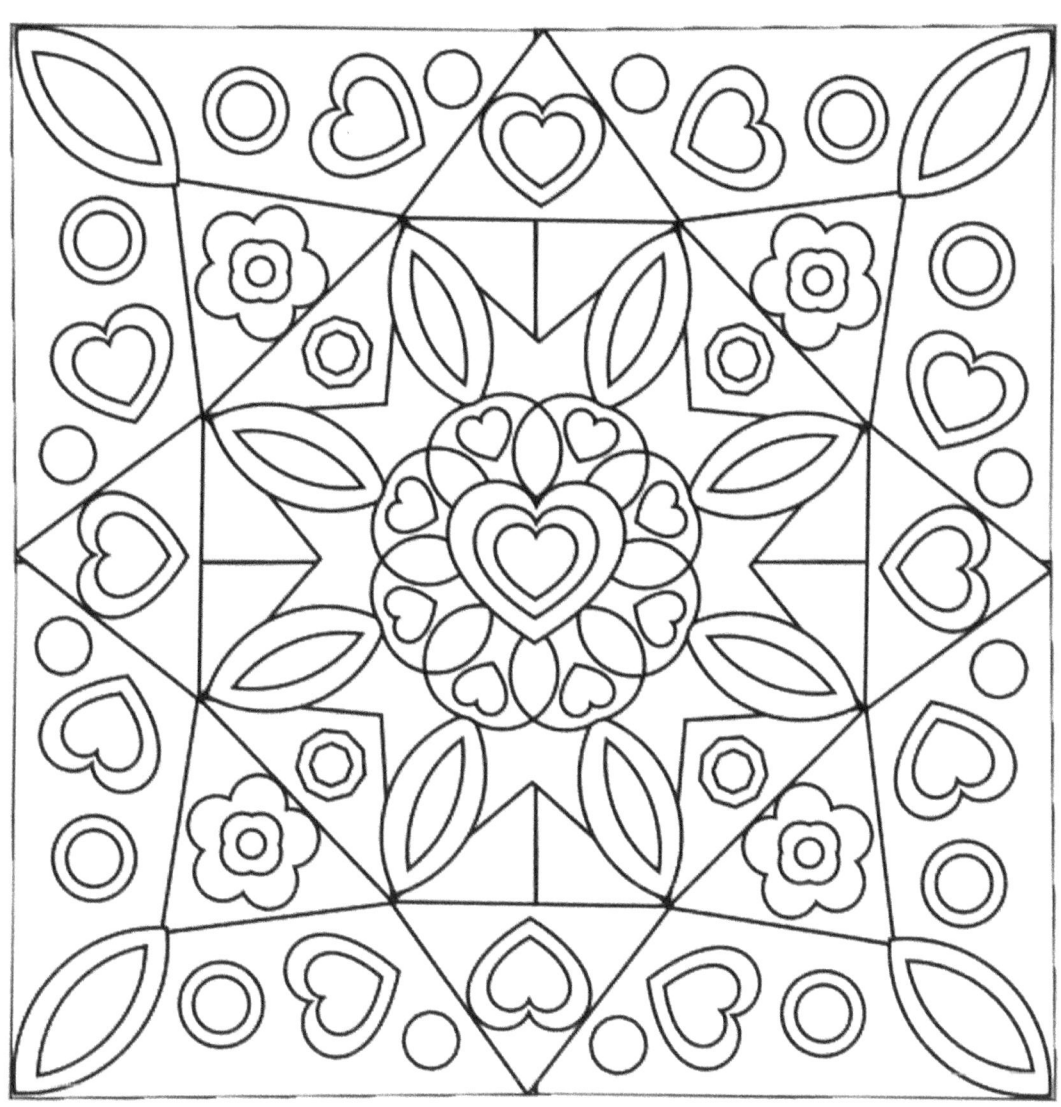

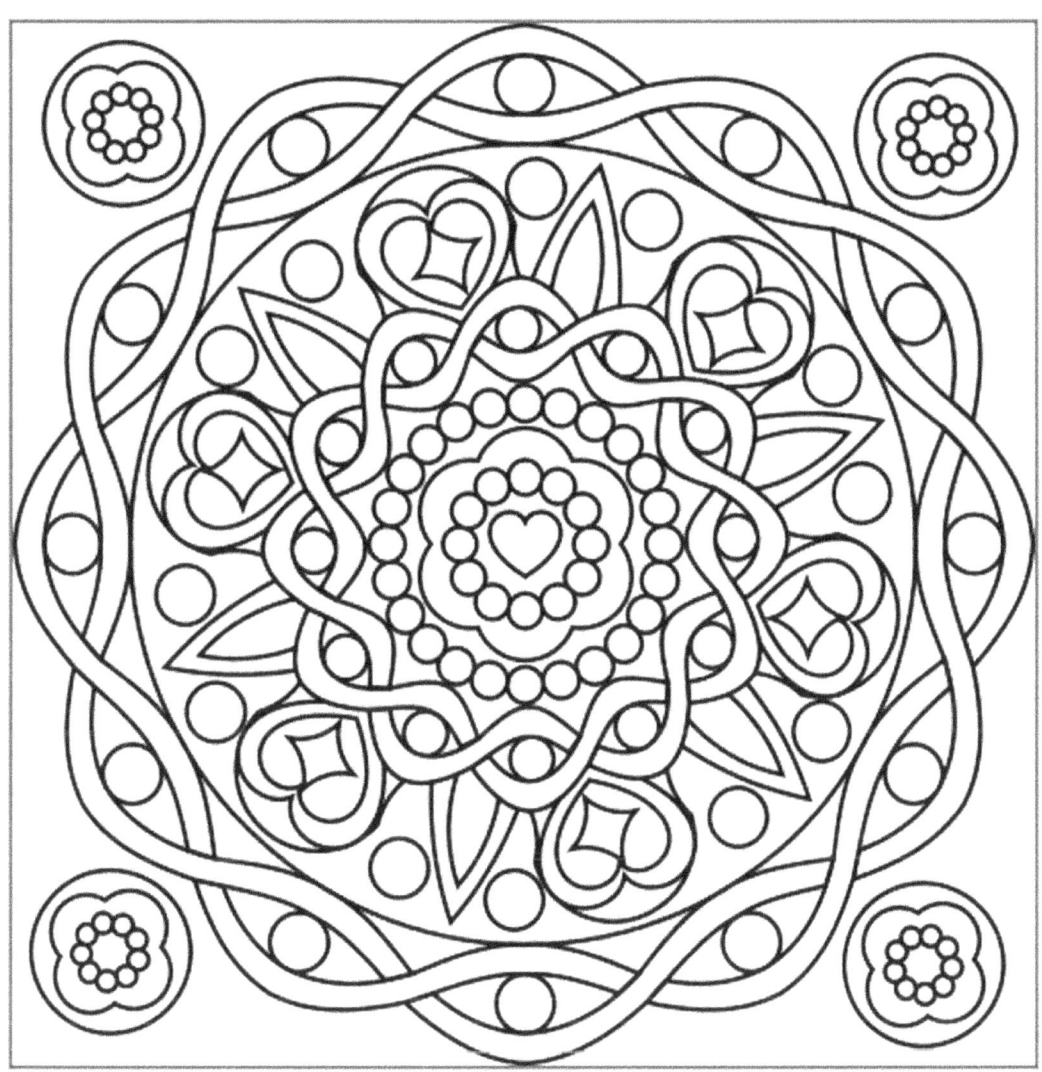

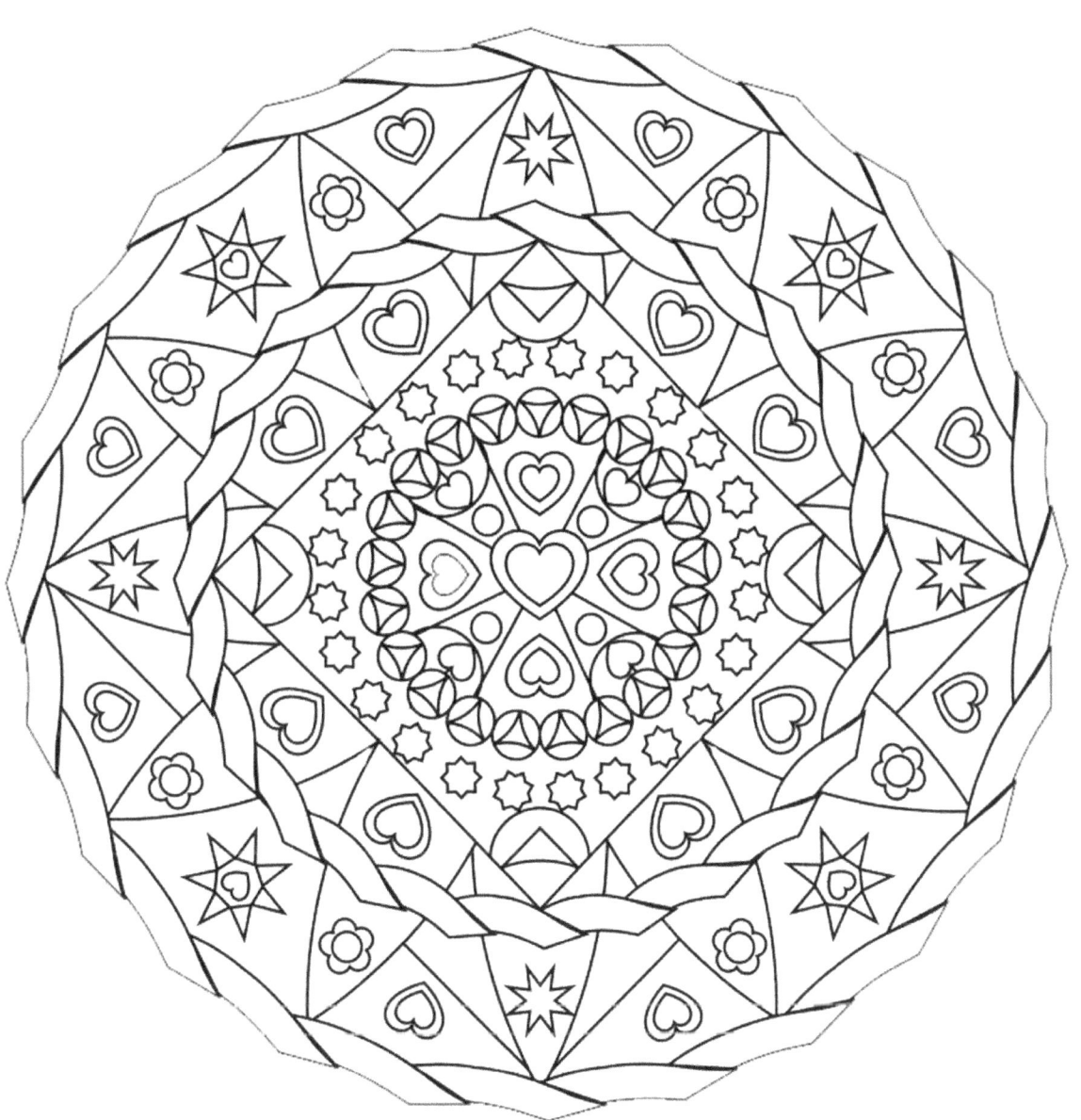

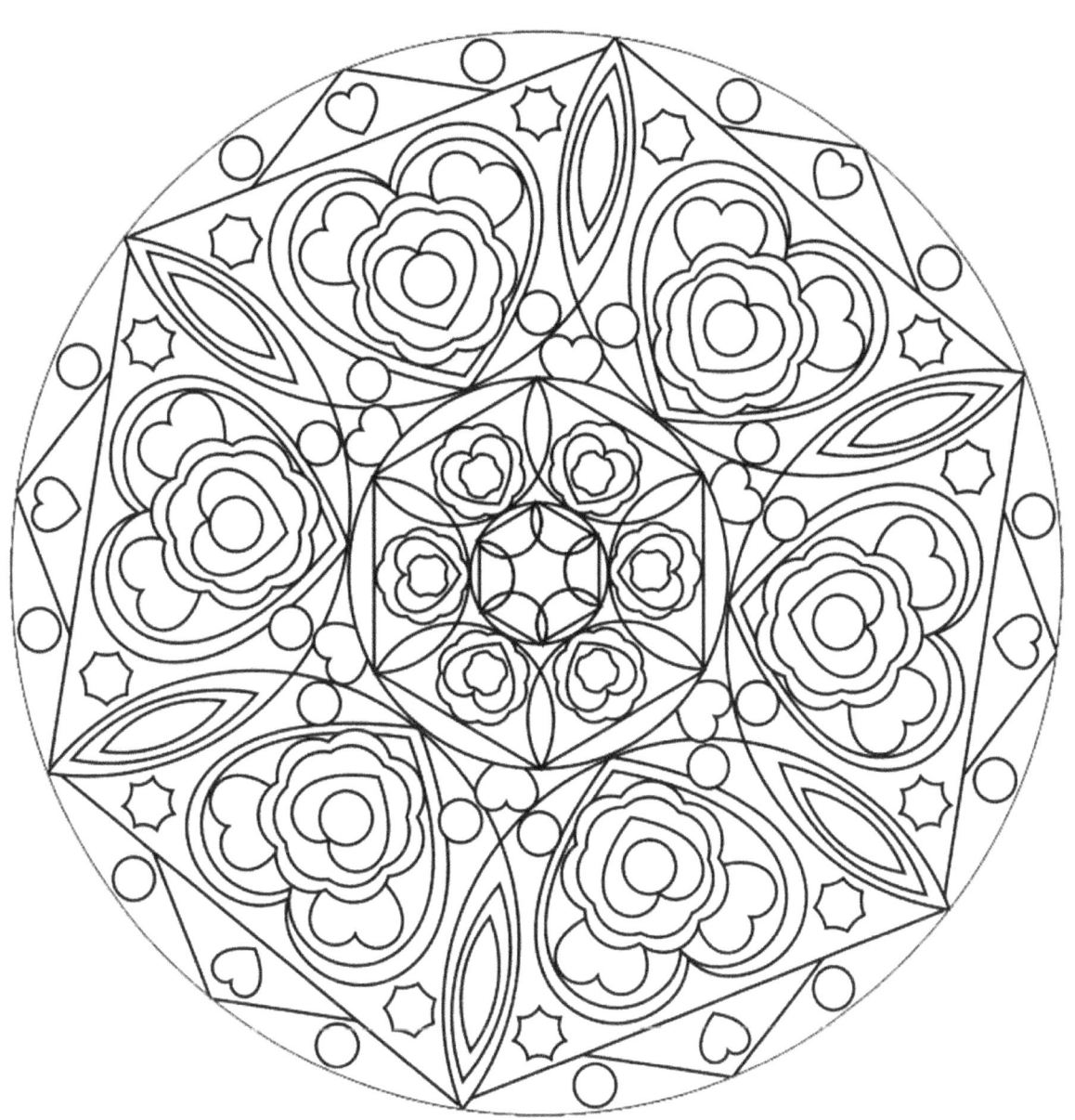

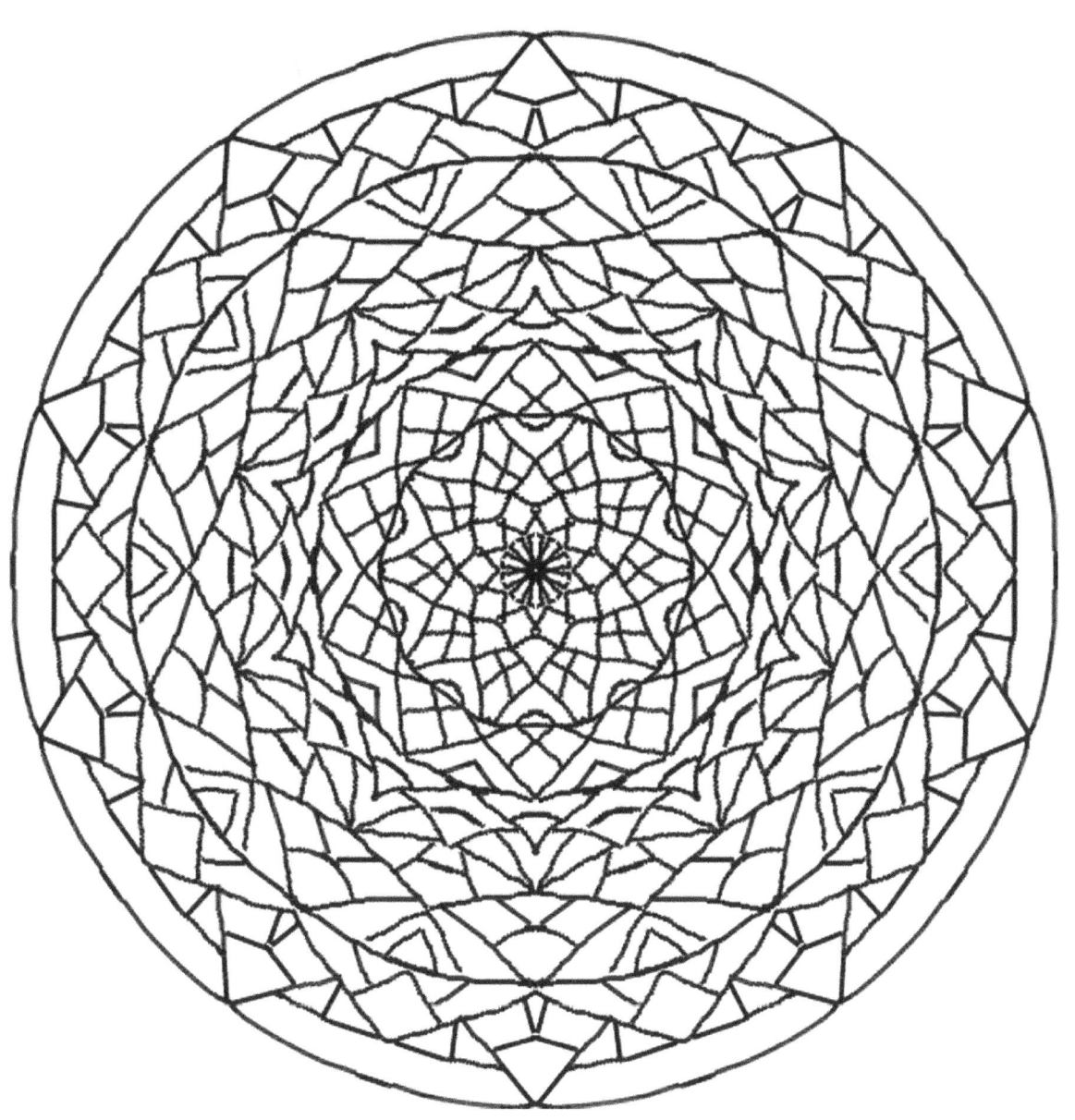

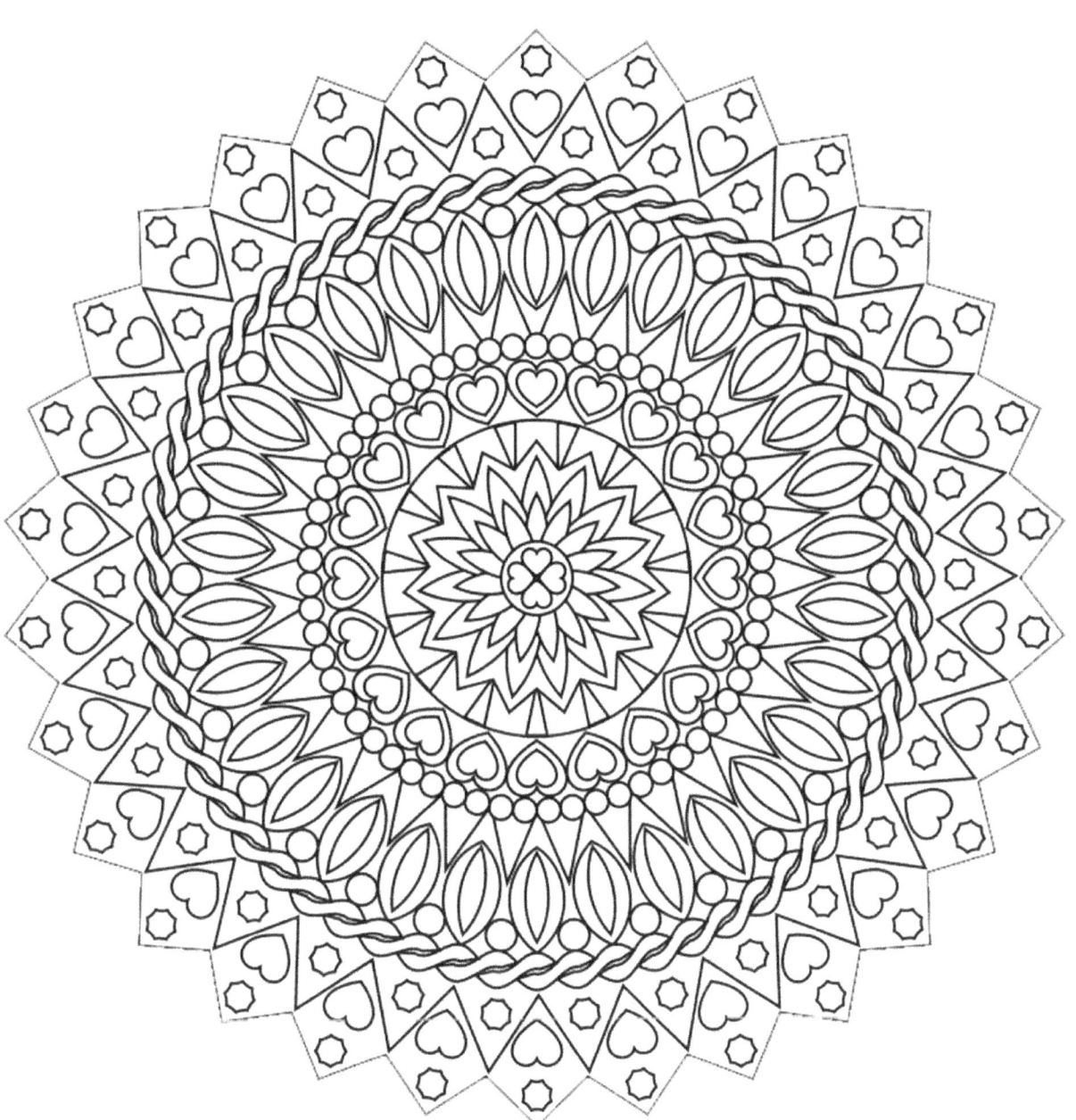

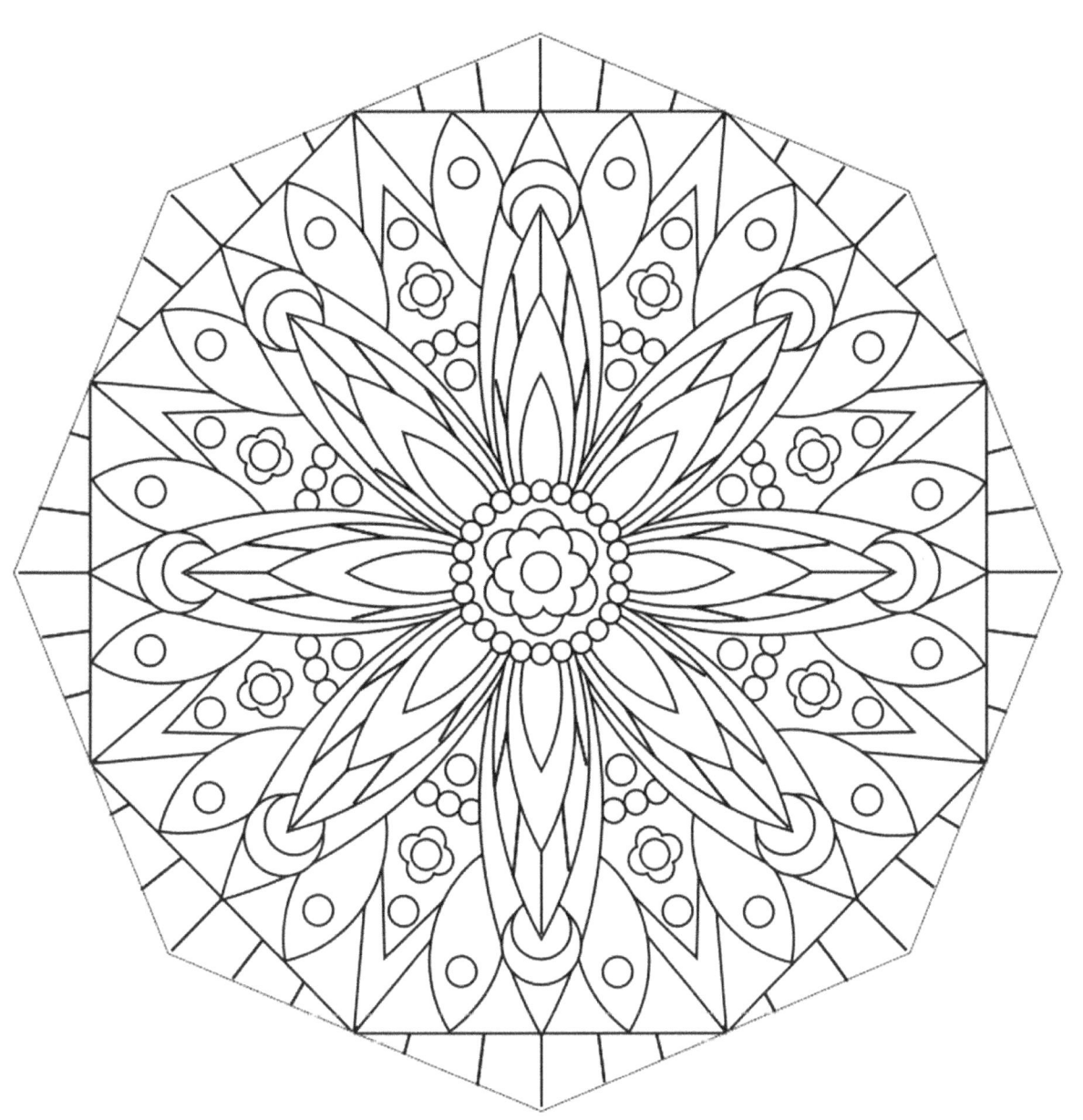

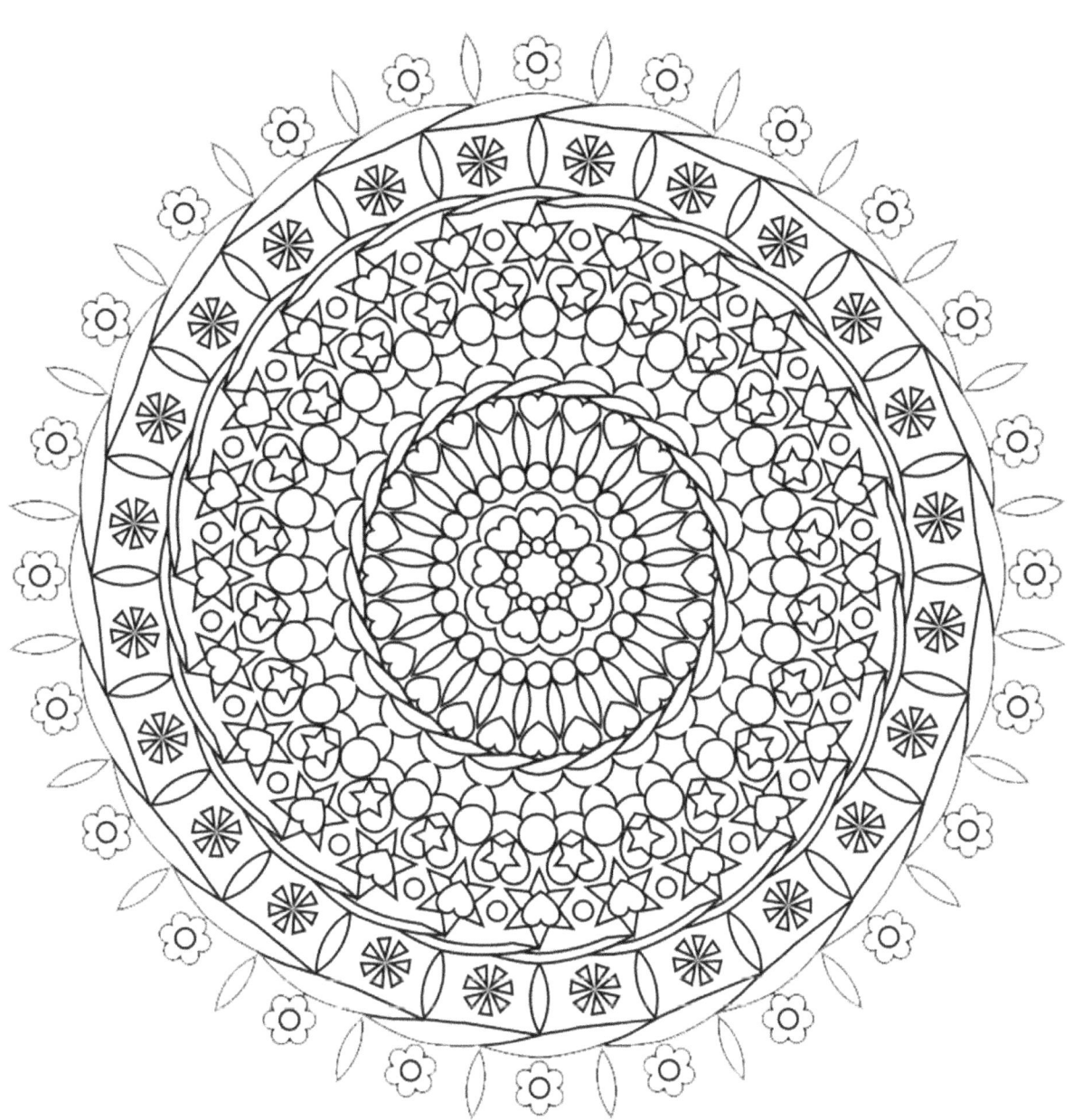

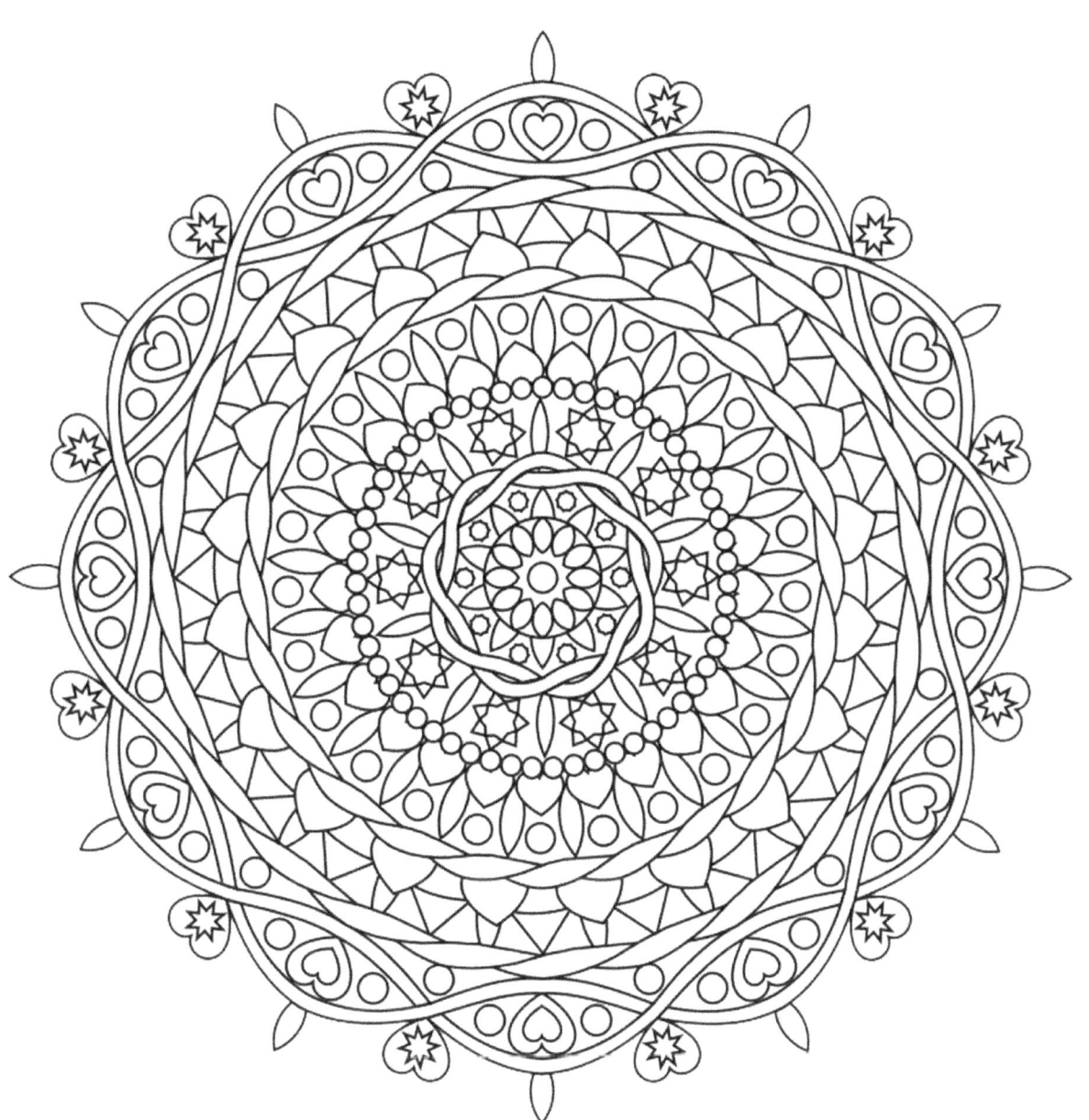

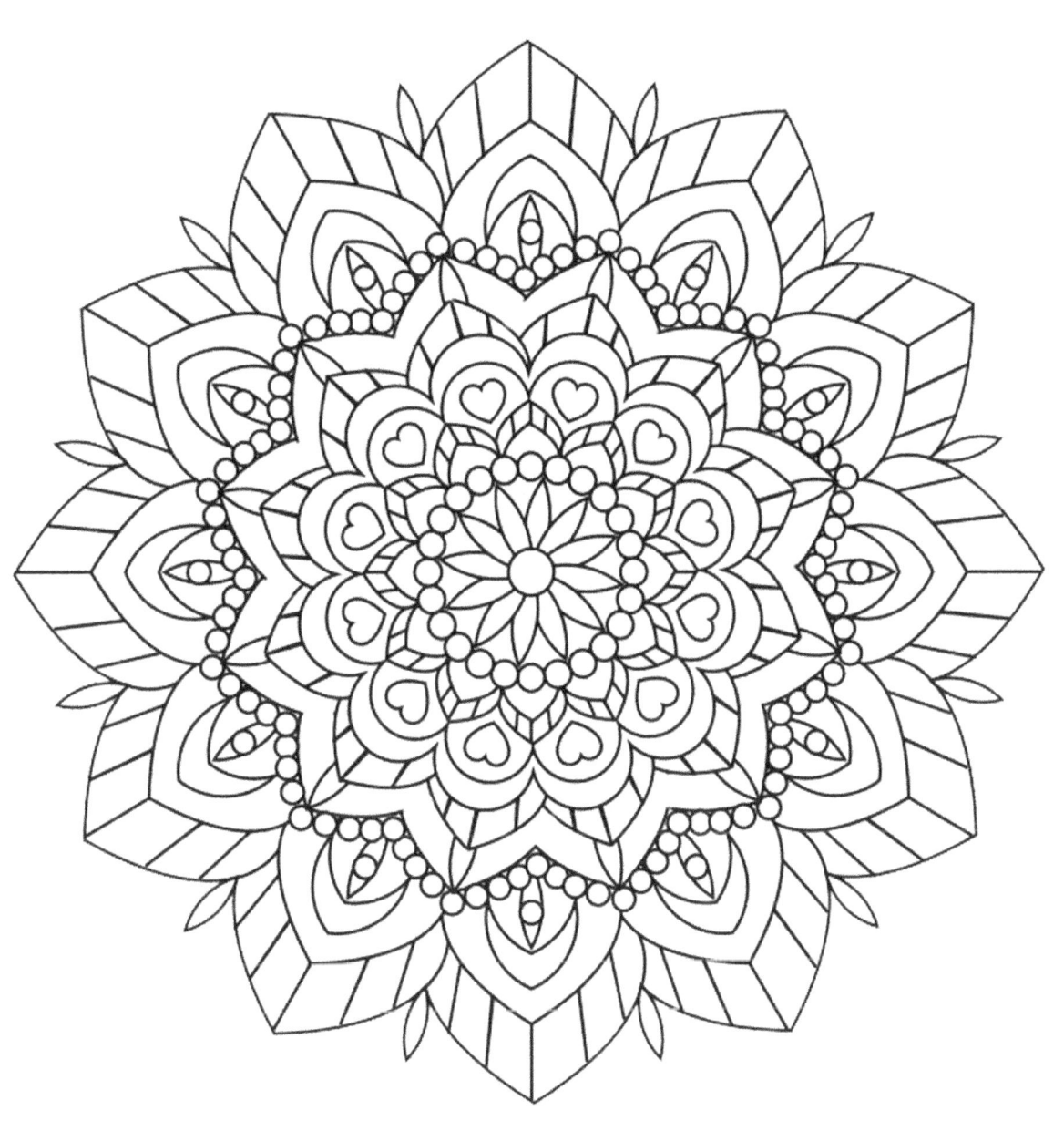

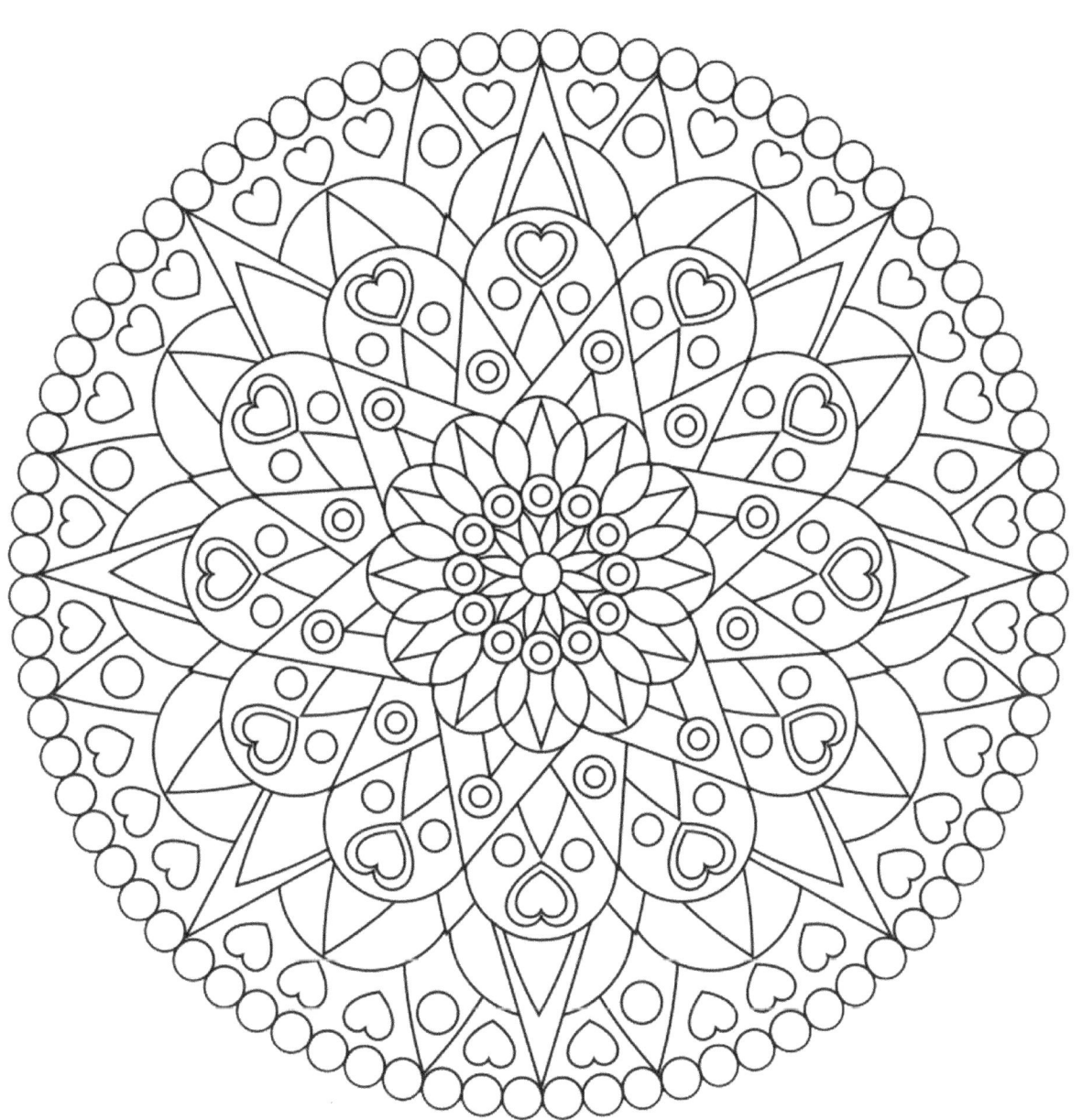

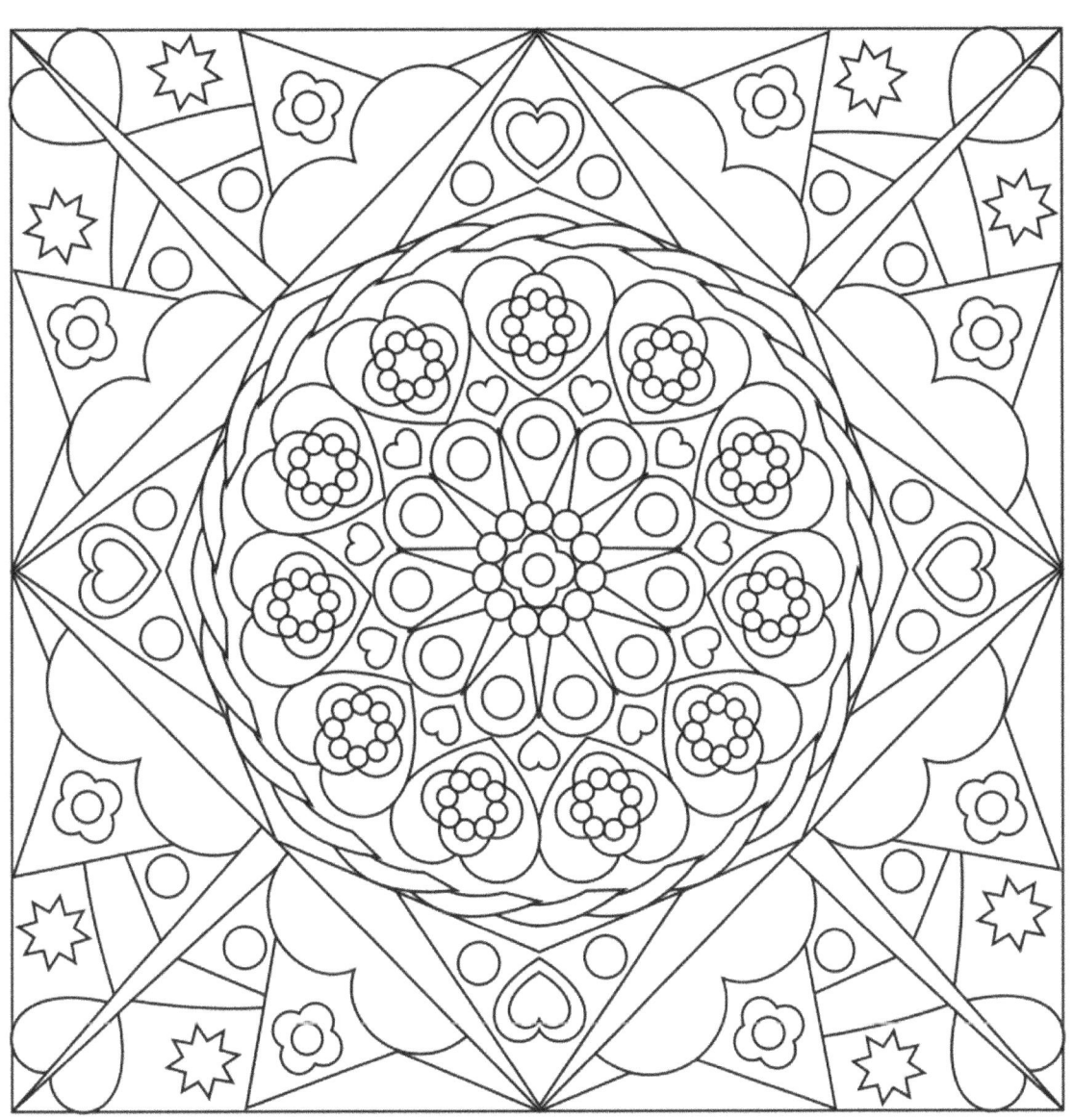

www.ingramcontent.com/pod-product-compliance
Lightning Source LLC
Chambersburg PA
CBHW081255180526
45170CB00007B/2435

* 9 7 8 1 5 4 2 4 7 8 2 3 6 *